MANAGEMENT DEVELOPMENT THROUGH JOB EXPERIENCES

AN ANNOTATED BIBLIOGRAPHY

MANAGEMENT DEVELOPMENT THROUGH JOB EXPERIENCES

AN ANNOTATED BIBLIOGRAPHY

Cynthia D. McCauley
Stéphane Brutus

Center for Creative Leadership
Greensboro, North Carolina

1998

The Center for Creative Leadership is an international, nonprofit educational institution founded in 1970 to advance the understanding, practice, and development of leadership for the benefit of society worldwide. As a part of this mission, it publishes books and reports that aim to contribute to a general process of inquiry and understanding in which ideas related to leadership are raised, exchanged, and evaluated. The ideas presented in its publications are those of the author or authors.

The Center thanks you for supporting its work through the purchase of this volume. If you have comments, suggestions, or questions about any Center publication, please contact John R. Alexander, President, at the address given below.

Center for Creative Leadership
Post Office Box 26300
Greensboro, North Carolina 27438-6300

CCL No. 337

Library of Congress Cataloging-in-Publication Data

McCauley, Cynthia D. (Cynthia Denise), 1958–
    Management development through job experiences : an annotated bibliography / Cynthia D. McCauley, Stéphane Brutus.
        p. cm.
    Includes bibliographical references.
    ISBN 1-882197-32-1
    1. Executives—Training of—Bibliography. 2. Experiential learning—Bibliography.
I. Brutus, Stéphane. II. Title.
Z7164.C81M337 1998
[HF5549.5.T7]
016.6584'07124—dc21   98-23154
                                                                              CIP

Table of Contents

Preface

In 1981 researchers at the Center for Creative Leadership (CCL), in collaboration with several corporations, launched a study focused on executive learning, growth, and change. At the heart of this research was an effort to understand key developmental experiences in managerial careers. This effort led to the publication of *The Lessons of Experience: How Successful Executives Develop on the Job* by Morgan McCall, Michael Lombardo, and Ann Morrison (Lexington Books, 1988). It also marked the beginning of CCL's continuing interest in management development through job experiences as an area of research and practice.

Since that time, CCL has sponsored further research on developmental assignments and how managers learn from them and has created tools for applying this knowledge to the practice of management development. We have supported others who have adopted the McCall, Lombardo, and Morrison "key events" methodology to study developmental events in particular subgroups of managers; this has added diversity to the organizational contexts in which learning from experience has been studied. We have also discovered kindred researchers who—using their own questions, methods, and frameworks—have enhanced our understanding of learning from job experiences. In addition, we have tried to understand how this concept of on-the-job development is related to other areas of inquiry, such as tacit knowledge, learning styles, and action learning. Finally, we have encouraged and observed efforts within organizations to create more developmental job experiences for managers and to stimulate more learning from these experiences.

This annotated bibliography is an attempt to bring together the resulting articles and publications from these various efforts—the stream of research connected to *The Lessons of Experience*, the larger body of research connected to on-the-job management development, other research topics that are related to learning from experience, and practices that stimulate on-the-job learning. We weren't interested in just compiling this information, however; we also wanted to show that the topic of management development through job experiences has emerged as an important field of inquiry. The following factors served as motivators in this effort:

- In our experience, even the people who have contributed to this body of knowledge (including ourselves) tend to be familiar with only pieces of it, and we would like to create a community that knows more about the whole. Such a community would foster cross-fertilization and allow for the integration of ideas.

- We want to attract more researchers to this field of inquiry. There is still much to learn. An annotated bibliography allows easier access for researchers newer to the field.
- Research can have more impact on practice if that research is part of a cumulative knowledge-building field. First, the weight of the evidence supporting research conclusions is stronger when the research is cumulative. For example, some practitioners who encounter the *Lessons of Experience* research ask somewhat skeptically, "But that was the 1980s. Is it still true?" We think that they will be less skeptical if they see an abundance of evidence about learning from experience coming from multiple studies over a number of years. Second, our understanding of a phenomenon is deepened when we try to integrate findings across numerous studies and researcher perspectives. This deeper understanding can lead to more detailed recommendations for practice.

Acknowledgments

We are especially indebted to the many researchers and trainers at CCL and others who have contributed to and shaped our collective knowledge about developmental assignments. We would like to specifically thank Victoria Marsick of Teacher's College at Columbia University; Morgan McCall of the Center for Effective Organizations at the University of Southern California; Jennifer Purdon of Merrill-Lynch Worldwide; and Ellen Van Velsor of CCL for their feedback on an earlier version of this bibliography. We also thank Christina Douglas of CCL for supplying our reference list with articles about action learning.

In addition, our thanks go to the CCL Publication Review Committee, whose members helped bring the manuscript to completion through their advice and support. The PRC members are: John Alexander, John Fleenor, Marcia Horowitz, Kelly Lombardino, Karen McNeil-Miller, Gordon Patterson, and Martin Wilcox.

Introduction

Development through job experiences—that is, managers learning, growing, and undergoing personal change as a result of the roles, responsibilities, and tasks they encounter in their jobs—has emerged as an important field of inquiry with a developed body of literature. Although on-the-job experiences have always been a powerful source of learning for managers, we have only been systematically studying them as a phenomenon for about fifteen years. The purpose of this annotated bibliography is to help illuminate this growing body of knowledge. It does so by providing information about selected books and articles that best reflect the streams of research and practice related to management development on the job.

The audience consists of those who want access to literature that has defined and informed this emerging field: researchers and practitioners who are already serious students in the field and are looking for additional sources of information, those who want their research to build on the existing knowledge base, and human resources practitioners for whom it is important to understand the research bases of on-the-job-development tools and practices.

This report is organized into three major sections. The first focuses on developmental jobs: their role in management development, what makes them developmental, and what is learned from them. The second is about the person in the job and how characteristics of the individual affect on-the-job development. Both of these sections contain research-based publications. The third section looks at management-development practices that use on-the-job development strategies. We include this section on practice for two reasons: Practice-oriented articles are another source of knowledge about the dynamics of on-the-job development, and such articles can serve as a stimulus for further research. Although works are included that describe applications and point out the implications for practice in research, we do not attempt to describe "best practices."

Each section contains five subsections: (1) an overview of the types of annotations contained in the section; (2) a summary of the key findings and implications in the literature; (3) future research directions; (4) annotations of the articles and books directly related to the topic of the section (a few publications that contain information relevant to more than one section are cross-referenced); and (5) a subsection called "Connections," containing lists of literature in other established domains, such as tacit knowledge and action learning, that can inform our understanding of management development through job experiences. In the section summaries, we refer to this literature and show how it is connected to our topic of interest. However, it is not within the scope of this bibliography to annotate the publications in these other domains.

Most of the literature on learning from job experiences is dealt with as a distinct source of management development, separate from learning from others (such as role models, bosses, mentors, or advisors)—even though these people are obviously a part of on-the-job experiences. We have maintained this distinction for the bibliography and thus have not included publications focused on learning from others. Part of the domain of other people as sources for workplace learning has been addressed in another recent CCL publication, *Formal Mentoring in Organizations: An Annotated Bibliography* by Christina A. Douglas (1997).

We used two main sources to find materials for inclusion in the bibliography. One was a pool of articles and books that had been collected over a period of fifteen years by CCL staff involved in research and application in this area; they found these articles through searches of the psychological and business literature, from their own reading in the field, or from colleagues who sent them material. The second source was a more systematic search of recent (1990-1996) articles in the *Psych-Lit* and *ABI-Inform* databases. In addition, during the compiling and writing process we added the most recent relevant works as they were released.

Our primary criterion for including an article or book in the bibliography was that it had contributed substantially to the body of knowledge on management development through job experiences. We also focused on work that is relatively current and accessible to most readers through libraries and bookstores. In doing our searches, we were mindful that various phrases have been used in the literature to refer to management development through job experiences—learning from experience, on-the-job learning, on-the-job development, developmental job experiences, stretch assignments, and developmental assignments—and adapted our search accordingly.

All of the annotated works and all of the references in the "Connections" sections are arranged by titles and authors in the two indexes at the end of this volume.

SECTION 1: DEVELOPMENTAL JOBS

Overview

This section contains articles and books related to the role job assignments play in management development, the characteristics of assignments that managers find particularly developmental, and how these assignments contribute to their development. The following conclusions are stressed: (1) job assignments play a central role in management development, (2) some types of jobs are more developmental than others, and (3) different kinds of developmental assignments are associated with different kinds of learning.

There are three major types of research articles annotated in this section: (1) studies in which managers describe previous developmental experiences in their careers, (2) studies that look at the developmental power of managers' current jobs, and (3) studies that examine how transitions to new jobs or work roles affect subsequent development. In general, this research takes a broad view of development, including not only the development of knowledge and skills (for instance, administrative, interpersonal, and strategic) but also the changes in perspectives and mental frameworks, such as ways of understanding self, one's role, one's relationship to others, and organizational systems.

Other research domains that inform our understanding of the role of jobs in management development include research on managers' tacit knowledge, work as a context for adult development, and employee participation in development activities, as well as a specific AT&T program of research that focused on the career progression of its managers.

We note here that we see a distinction between our primary interest—the role jobs play in long-term management development—and research that has examined how a manager learns or masters his or her new job. The former is focused on how managers' skills and perspectives are changed because of what they have to deal with in the job. These skills and perspectives become part of the person's managerial capacity and are taken to the next job. The latter is focused on how managers learn what their new job entails and what is expected of them, and how they diagnose and solve the problems they encounter in a new job. This type of learning is specific to the situation and will have to be repeated each time a new job is encountered.

Certainly there are connections between mastering a new job and developing as a manager. For example, in mastering a new job one learns about others' expectations of performance in the job; this may lead to a broader understanding of work roles that the manager takes with him or her to future assignments. Or diagnosing and solving a specific problem in an assignment can lead to improved problem-solving skills. But the "learning the job" research rarely looks at how a manager changes or grows as a manager because of his or her mastery of the specific situations and problems encountered in a job move. Because of the potential connections there, references to this literature are included.

Key Findings and Implications

Job assignments play a central role in management development.
Experience as a key component of learning has long been a part of adult learning theories (Dewey, 1938[1]; Knowles, 1970[2]; Kolb, 1984). However, until the 1980s, management development in the U.S. was synonymous with training. Adult learning theory was recognized, but its application was primarily in the realm of "How can we make training programs more experiential?"

It took several major studies in the 1980s (Broderick, 1983; McCall, Lombardo, & Morrison, 1988; Morrison, White, & Van Velsor, 1987, 1992; Wick, 1989; Zemke, 1985) to hit home the point that on-the-job experiences were *the* primary source of learning and development for managers. These studies had several things in common: (1) they collected data from fairly large numbers of successful executives; (2) they asked executives to reflect on their past, identifying key sources of learning and development in their careers; (3) they found that managers saw most of their learning occurring from the challenges encountered in their jobs and from influential people in their work settings (such as bosses, mentors, and role models)—formal training programs and nonwork experiences contributed to a less extent; and (4) their findings were influential in part because they were based on powerful stories from executives themselves.

Although these larger studies may have drawn more attention, there were other research projects and applications that supported their findings:

• *AT&T Longitudinal Studies of Managers* (Bray, Campbell, & Grant, 1974; Bray & Howard, 1983; Howard & Bray, 1988). Begun in the 1950s, this research effort tracked a group of managers from several Bell Systems operating companies, assessing their skills, interests, personality, and

---

[1] John Dewey. *Experience and education.* West Lafayette, IN: Kappa Delta Pi, 1938.

[2] Malcolm S. Knowles. *The modern practice of adult education.* New York: Association Press, 1970.

progress at multiple points in time. Amount of job challenge experienced by the managers was an important predictor of advancement into middle management. For example, sixty-one percent of the college recruits who were predicted to fail to reach middle management actually made it to middle management eight years later if they had high job challenge. Of those predicted to reach middle management, but who experienced low job challenge, only thirty percent actually reached it. Thus, although this study did not assess the degree to which managers were learning from their jobs, it does suggest that challenging job experiences play a critical role in managerial success.

• *American Management Association's survey of CEOs* (Margerison & Kakabadse, 1984). As part of this survey, over 700 CEOs rated the impact of 21 "key influences" on their own career development. Although the list contained a mixture of personal attributes, skills, experiences, and relationships, several of the highly ranked influences were job experiences, such as taking on the challenge of a senior role and early overall responsibility for important tasks.

• *Management development in the U.K.* Before the major U.S. studies were done, British management development researchers and practitioners were actively engaged in work on job experiences as the basis for learning and development. Davies and Easterby-Smith (1984) were among the first to systematically analyze the characteristics of developmental jobs. Revans (1980) developed *action learning*, a management development strategy that utilized work on real organizational problems; Stewart (1984) advocated the use of radical job moves for development; and Mumford (1980) wrote practical advice to help managers capitalize on their jobs as learning opportunities.

• *Research on tacit knowledge* (Sternberg, Wagner, Williams, & Horvath, 1995). Sternberg and his colleagues developed the notion of tacit knowledge—knowledge that is developed through direct experience as one moves from a novice to an expert in a given field or domain—as a type of knowledge distinct from that acquired through formal education. The degree of tacit knowledge about business management was found to be related to managerial success. Although the way in which managers acquire tacit knowledge has not been looked at closely, studies of this phenomenon do support the notion that, in order to be successful, managers need to develop increasingly complex levels of expertise.

• *Work as a context for adult development.* Several adult development theorists (Basseches, 1984; Kegan, 1994; Torbert, 1987) have emphasized the workplace as a setting for continued moral, cognitive, and interpersonal development in adulthood. The challenges faced, particularly by managers, in the modern organization are seen as the stimuli for reexamining one's worldview and developing more complex frameworks for guiding decisions and actions.

In addition to this related work, the key finding from the major studies—that on-the-job experiences are the primary source of learning and development for managers—has been replicated within specific companies (Valerio, 1990) and with managers of total quality efforts (Favorite, 1994), entrepreneurs (Reuber & Fischer, 1993), R&D managers (Pearson & McCauley, 1991), public service executives (Little, 1991), and public school principals (Perry, 1994).

The major implication of this finding is that the task of developing managers involves much more than formal education and training; the key emphasis in management development systems should be on learning through job assignments. Likewise, an important aspect of making decisions about which manager to place in a job is how the assignment will challenge that individual and contribute to his or her growth.

Some types of jobs are more developmental than others.

Although the tasks and challenges encountered on the job are a major source of learning for managers, all jobs are not created developmentally equal. Managers report some kinds of jobs as having more impact on their learning than others. As noted earlier, there are three kinds of studies that help delineate the characteristics of more developmental jobs: (1) studies in which managers describe developmental experiences in their careers (Davies & Easterby-Smith, 1984; Favorite, 1994; Isabella & Forbes, 1994; Lindsey, Homes, & McCall, 1987; Little, 1991; McCall et al., 1988; Morrison et al., 1992; Perry, 1994; Reuber & Fischer, 1993, 1994; Valerio, 1990; Wick, 1989); (2) studies in which managers rate characteristics of their current job and then correlate these ratings with some measure of learning (Kelleher, Finestone, & Lowy, 1986; McCauley, Ohlott, & Ruderman, 1989; McCauley, Ruderman, Ohlott, & Morrow, 1994; Ruderman, Ohlott, & McCauley, 1990); and (3) studies that examine how transitions to new jobs or work roles affect personal change or development (Beck, 1988; Brett, 1983; Hall, 1986; Hill, 1992; Nicholson & West, 1988).

Taken as a whole, these studies would suggest three broad characteristics of developmental assignments. A fourth characteristic is found primarily in the qualitative descriptions of past experiences. The terms *challenging* and *stretching* have often been used to describe assignments that are developmental. The characteristics below help delineate what is meant by a challenging or stretching assignment.

 1. *Transitions that put the manager in new situations with unfamiliar responsibilities* (Beck, 1988; Brett, 1982; Davies & Easterby-Smith, 1984; Hall, 1986; Hill, 1992; Isabella & Forbes, 1993; Little, 1991; McCall et al., 1988; McCauley et al., 1989, 1994; Morrison et al., 1992; Nicholson & West, 1988; Perry, 1994; Ruderman et al., 1990; Valerio, 1990; Wick, 1989). Having to face new situations with unfamiliar responsibilities is most frequently the outcome of a job move (for instance, promotion or move to a new business, function, organization, or location), but can come from expanded responsibilities within the same job or the redefinition of a job due to reorganization or changes in the external environment. New and unfamiliar situations provide an opportunity to learn because they disrupt routines, call for new skills and behaviors, and yield surprises that cause the manager to reexamine assumptions.

It is important to note that a novel work situation does not automatically lead to development; many job moves are not experienced as developmental. If there are few new elements in the job (Davies & Easterby-Smith, 1984; McCauley et al., 1989; Nicholson & West, 1988), little increase in the amount of discretion the manager has to define the job (Brett, 1992), or if differences from previous positions go unnoticed by the incumbent (Brett, 1992; Nicholson & West, 1988), the job move will tend to be experienced as less developmental.

 2. *Tasks or projects that require the manager to bring about change or build relationships* (Davies & Easterby-Smith, 1984; Favorite, 1994; Hill, 1992; Kelleher et al., 1986; Little, 1991; McCall et al., 1988; McCauley et al., 1989, 1994; Morrison et al., 1992; Perry, 1994; Reuber & Fischer, 1993, 1994; Ruderman et al., 1990; Valerio, 1990; Zemke, 1985). Managers are involved in creating change when they are fixing problems or when they are starting a new initiative. They work with others in various ways: leading subordinates; influencing bosses; collaborating or competing with peers; and negotiating with, persuading, and serving outsiders.

Creating change and building relationships is the primary work of managers; thus developing management expertise requires doing the work of managers. To do this work, they must take action—a necessary component of the on-the-job learning process. The more complex and uncertain the change efforts are, the more difficult and diverse the working relationships are, and the bigger the learning challenges of the job.

3. *High-responsibility, high-latitude jobs* (Basseches, 1984; Davies & Easterby-Smith, 1984; Isabella & Forbes, 1994; Kelleher et al., 1986; McCall et al., 1990; McCauley et al., 1994; Morrison et al., 1992; Reuber & Fischer, 1993; Ruderman et al., 1990; Wick, 1989). In these types of jobs, managers have responsibility for discrete areas of the business, have profit-and-loss responsibility, or make decisions that can have a major impact on the organization. Managers in these types of jobs generally are also given a high degree of latitude in their initiatives and discretion in their decision making.

High-responsibility, high-latitude jobs offer developmental opportunities for a number of reasons: (1) Managers in such positions deal with complex systems and have to make decisions that require balancing priorities and making trade-offs. Such experiences give them the opportunity to better understand the interrelatedness of systems and to integrate various perspectives. (2) The consequences of their decisions matter. This factor can cause managers to explore issues more deeply and be more cognizant of actions and their intended consequences. (3) They have some freedom to experiment. They are less likely to be constrained by set routines and procedures and can thus test out their understanding of a situation by taking actions and seeing the consequences.

4. *Negative experiences* (Kelleher et al., 1986; Little, 1991; McCall et al., 1988; Morrison et al., 1992; Reuber & Fischer, 1993; Ruderman et al., 1990; Valerio, 1990). Negative experiences include business failures and setbacks, problematic working relationships, demotions or missed promotions, and exhaustion due to work overload. The contribution of negative experiences to one's development is generally acknowledged only in retrospective accounts of developmental experiences, although learning particular kinds of lessons (such as acceptance of politics as a part of organizational life, the scope of personal limits, and recognizing blind spots) have been associated with negative experiences in the current job.

Negative experiences can promote learning when they stimulate action to alleviate the source of the stress that they cause (for example, trying to improve relationships or change management style), or they trigger self-reflection. Because this reflection often occurs after the experience, it is not surprising that we find more reports of learning from these experiences in retrospective reports.

Research that has helped to delineate the characteristics of developmental assignments has two main implications: (1) Organizations need to be aware of what kinds of jobs in their organizations have higher developmental potential so that they can use these assignments as part of their management development system. Depending on the system, these assignments might be targeted for high-potential managers, for managers being prepared for particular roles, for managers taking part in formal development programs, or for some other subset of managers. (2) At the same time, most managerial jobs can be shaped to increase their developmental potential so that all managers have developmental aspects to their work. Major job moves represent only one option by which developmental assignments can be created. Novelty, change-oriented tasks, relationship-building tasks, and responsibility coupled with latitude can be nurtured within jobs.

Another important factor in this research should be noted: Although we talk about the characteristics of developmental jobs as if they are objective features that could be listed in a job description, all of the research in this area relies on the manager to describe his or her job experiences. Thus, we are actually talking about the job as *experienced* by the manager rather than an objective reality. The same job given to different managers could have different characteristics. Managers bring different experiences to the job; what is new or unfamiliar to one manager may not be to another. Managers often shape their jobs; one may embark on a mission of change whereas another decides to maintain stability. Managers interpret their jobs; one manager may see that he or she has wide latitude in making decisions whereas another sees only constraints. Thus, although an organization can identify types of jobs as having developmental potential, when making a specific person-job match, it needs to ascertain whether a particular job at a particular time has developmental potential for that manager. It also should help shape the manager's understanding of the developmental features of the job.

Different kinds of developmental assignments are associated with different kinds of learning.

The relationship between learning particular lessons (for instance, how to delegate effectively, broaden perspectives on the business, or how to work with senior executives) and characteristics of assignments do not appear to be random (Favorite, 1994; Lindsey, Homes, & McCall, 1987; Little, 1991; McCall et al., 1988; McCauley, Eastman, & Ohlott, 1995; Reuber & Fischer, 1994; Ruderman et al., 1990; Valerio, 1990; Van Velsor & Hughes, 1990).

At the most basic level, the connection between assignments and learning can be understood as "you learn what you're practicing." Thus, managers learn how to handle subordinate performance problems from having to confront a problem subordinate. They learn about long-range planning from assignments at corporate headquarters. They learn the strategies and tactics of negotiation when they have to negotiate. School principals learn that good relationships with parents are important from their experiences (both successful and unsuccessful) working with parents.

At the next level, there are some learning themes associated with the four broad characteristics described above:

Characteristic	Area of Learning
New situations with unfamiliar responsibilities	• broader perspective • willingness to rely on others • business and technical knowledge • dealing with ambiguity
Creating change and building relationships	• willingness to take full responsibility for a group or project • negotiation skills • how to achieve cooperation • ability to see others' perspectives • willingness to involve others in decisions
High responsibility and latitude	• decisiveness • decision-making and organizing skills • ability to see the "big picture"
Negative experiences	• awareness of limits and shortcomings • how to cope with stressful situations • motivation to take charge of own career

Finally, there are a few things, like self-confidence, increased perseverance, and ability to motivate employees, that seem to come from many types of assignments.

The finding that different kinds of assignments lead to different kinds of learning has two main implications: (1) Variety in assignments throughout one's career is important for developing broad perspectives and a large repertoire of skills. Managers who have faced and learned from the demands in different types of assignments will be more versatile. (2) Although giving a manager a new challenge is a good general strategy for continuous development, when a particular skill or competency is targeted to a manager's developmental need, then seeking out a particular kind of assignment will provide the optimum opportunities for developing in that area. For example, if a manager needs to learn to rely on others more, then a new responsibility outside of the manager's area of expertise gives him or her the opportunity to practice relying on others. Or if a manager needs to improve his or her ability to gain cooperation with other groups, then an assignment that required relationship-building would be optimal.

Research Directions

Two things stand out about the methodology used in research on developmental jobs: (1) For the most part, it relies on retrospective reports of previous jobs or descriptions of current jobs; very little longitudinal research is available. Thus, we know little about how development unfolds over time within a job or about how managers' attributions of what was learned from an assignment may change as they become more distanced in time from the assignment. We also know little about how the sequencing of jobs or assignments might affect long-term career development. (2) The methodology relies entirely on self-reports of job features and on-the-job learning. The degree to which challenges experienced by a job incumbent are recognizable to bosses, co-workers, or human resources professionals in the organization is unknown. This is an important question for management-development systems that rely on non-job-incumbents to identify developmental assignments and place managers in them. Also, we do not know whether those who work with the manager would agree that he or she has learned or changed as a result of an assignment. Does what the manager thinks he or she has learned manifest itself in ways their co-workers can see?

Another issue that is unclear from the literature is the degree to which assignments that have been experienced as developmental were self-initiated. Several studies did find that self-initiation was often a characteristic of moves to more developmental jobs (Davies & Easterby-Smith, 1984; Wick, 1989), but most are silent on this topic. Although it is often encouraged in the literature, we do not know the impact of an increased role by the organization in orchestrating developmental assignments. Will the dynamics of the experience change for the manager? Will more managers experience their jobs as developmental, or will only those subsets of managers who are particularly motivated to learn (and thus would initiate their own learning opportunities) benefit from the assignments?

An additional facet that is touched on in only a few studies is the organizational context within which assignments are embedded. Davies and Easterby-Smith (1984) found that managers in stable organizations that possessed dominant positions in their markets reported less development than did managers in more turbulent organizations. Kelleher et al. (1986) found managerial learning to be positively associated with the degree to which the organizational context supported learning, such as having an atmosphere in which innovation is encouraged. This view is emphasized by others doing research on job assignments (Brett, 1982; Hall, 1986; Hill, 1992; McCall et al., 1988; McCauley et al., 1989; Zemke, 1985). Challenging jobs are particularly difficult, taking managers outside their comfort zones and putting them at risk of failure. To embrace a challenge and learn from it, managers need to also experience encouragement and support in their assignments. More understanding of the impact of organizational turbulence and organizational support is needed.

Finally, questions remain that concern whether the developmental features of assignments will change as managerial work changes (for example, requiring more cross-functional work, more participation from employees, more interactions with diverse people, keeping pace with rapid technological changes). Certainly the specific challenges in assignments will change, but a broader question is whether these challenges will continue to fall within the categories of unfamiliar responsibilities, creating change, building relationships, high responsibility and latitude, and negative experiences, or whether new categories will emerge. These new challenges may also trigger learning in domains not previously experienced by managers. Thus, research on developmental jobs needs to keep pace with major changes in managerial roles and responsibilities.

Annotations

Section 1.1: Developmental Experiences in Managerial Careers

Richard Broderick. How Honeywell teaches its managers to manage. *Training,* January 1983, pp. 18-23.

Because Honeywell, Inc., did not feel it was doing enough to develop or recruit managers, its corporate human-resources development department established a task force to study the process by which the company was developing its managers. The task force surveyed 300 managers from throughout the corporation; all of these managers were perceived as effective. The goal was to find out what it was that managers learned at different levels and phases of their careers and how they learned it. Through the survey they learned that only a small fraction of an individual's management techniques were learned in the classroom. It came as a surprise to the task force that about eighty percent of learning came from contact with key people in the workplace and from on-the-job experiences.

The resulting Honeywell management development model is three-dimensional. It identifies the development needs of managers at five levels in the organization (from pre-supervisor to vice president and higher), at four development phases (entry, skill-building, performance, and mastery), which can be achieved through three development strategies (education, relationships, and job).

Julia Davies and Mark Easterby-Smith. Learning and developing from managerial work experiences. *Journal of Management Studies*, 21:2, 1984, pp. 169-183.

The issue addressed in this article is whether managers learn and develop as much as they might from their normal work experiences. The information is based on an analysis of sixty interviews with middle- and senior-level managers from five different companies. They were asked questions about their developmental experiences.

Managers from two of the companies reported substantially less development than did those from the other three. Companies in which development occurred less frequently had stable environments and possessed dominant positions in their respective markets. The companies whose managers reported more development had more turbulent environments. A few managers in non-developing cultures did report high levels of development. However, this development seemed to be a function of organizational factors because of the managers' specific positions within their organizations—in boundary roles, such as marketing and public relations, and in newly established departments.

The kinds of experiences across the companies that led to development were described in more detail. About half of the experiences were the result of a job move and half occurred within existing jobs. Developmental job moves tended to have three features: (1) they presented a significant element completely new to the manager that prevented him or her from using tactics and routines that had worked in previous jobs, (2) they involved responsibility for a discrete area of business, requiring decision making under conditions of risk and uncertainty and then subsequent implementation of the resulting plan, and (3) the moves were self-initiated by the manager, perhaps making them riskier than organizationally initiated moves. Many job moves, however, were not experienced as developmental. These moves were perceived as "more of the same."

Developmental experiences within existing jobs occurred primarily due to changes taking place in and around the manager's job (such changes as in the external business environment and reorganizations). Managers who were able to take advantage of these situations seemed to be in roles that were not tightly defined; they had freedom to operate outside the constraints of existing systems and procedures. A smaller number of developmental experiences within existing jobs were the result of special assignments given to the manager, such as being assigned to a start-up project or given a troubleshooting role.

The authors point out a number of implications of the findings: (1) if a manager is to develop within a job, it is important that he or she has freedom to evolve the job in response to changing circumstances; (2) organizations should selectively reduce the filters that protect managers from change; (3) organizations need guidelines around promotion and selection decisions to help them override the risk-aversive tendency to minimize the amount of novelty the new manager will experience; (4) promotions should not be viewed as the only path for development, but rather development can be seen as occurring within existing jobs; and (5) there needs to be support within organizations for managers who are working to change, including access to mentors.

Bonnie B. Favorite. *Becoming a total quality leader: Developmental experiences of executives responsible for total quality management.* Doctoral dissertation, 1994, North Carolina State University, Raleigh.

This study sought to determine which on-the-job experiences were likely to contribute to the success of an individual who is responsible for leading an exemplary quality effort and what lessons these individuals may attach to these key events. Interviews were conducted with ten people who had led quality efforts in companies that had won the Malcolm Baldrige National Quality Award. The primary interview question was modeled after the "key event" question in the McCall, Lombardo, and Morrison (1988) research on critical learning events in managerial careers; the question was modified to focus on key events that had made a difference in the manager's approach to leading in the context of total quality management.

Five categories of events were identified: challenging projects, role models, benchmarking, training and education, and feedback. Challenging projects and role models were the most frequently mentioned types of events. Seven lesson themes were identified: commitment, empowerment, conceptual understanding of quality, team orientation, systems perspective, resourcefulness, and communication. A number of the events and lessons were similar to those reported by managers in previous studies; however, benchmarking as a critical event and conceptual understanding of quality as an important lesson theme reflected the particular environment within which the respondents in this study operated—the context of total quality management.

Lynn A. Isabella and Ted Forbes. *The interpersonal side of careers: How key events impact executive careers.* Paper presented at the annual meeting of the Academy of Management, Dallas, TX, 1994.

This investigation focused on the events that shape executive careers, with particular emphasis on how executives make sense of their own careers. The term *subjective career,* coined in the late 1960s, refers to the meanings that individuals attribute to their careers. The use of managers' introspection on their careers can be employed in conjunction with more objective methods of career assessment. The authors argue that managers' interpretations of their careers leads to a better understanding of the whole career experience.

In-depth interviews of forty-one managers yielded six categories of events that were perceived as critical by managers: educational experiences, family situations, new jobs or career directions, promotions/projects, interaction with significant individuals, and personal crises. The meaning and significance that managers derived from these experiences were classified into four categories: milestones, confirmational events, decisional events, and transformational events.

Milestones mark a significant achievement or turning point in an individual's career, such as graduation or a first job. A confirmational event authenticates one's self-concept and self-awareness. Decisional events, such as starting a new business, fall within the control of the individual and are accompanied by delayed rewards. Transformational events, while not necessarily traumatic, are associated with a major overhaul of values and priorities and important changes in one's career.

Certain patterns emerged as to how individuals categorized their career events in one or another categories. For example, a portion of the managers reported a majority of milestone events; these individuals interpreted most of their significant career events as turning points. The authors state that individuals view their careers and their past experiences through four distinct mind-sets: instrumental, incremental, challenge, and learning.

The instrumental mind-set is characterized by a linear view of one's career. Each career event is related to the one before and is a necessary predecessor for events to follow. The incremental mind-set involves a sense of gradual broadening of one's competencies. Although it shares the linearity of the instrumental mind-set, there is a sense of incremental expansion rather than following a specific path. Individuals with the challenge mind-set perceived each key event as an opportunity to test new skills, try new approaches, and take risks. Finally, the learning mind-set was found in individuals who perceived each key event as part of a larger development pattern. This mind-set was characterized by a continuous sense of ongoing learning and transformation.

Esther H. Lindsey, Virginia Homes, and Morgan W. McCall, Jr. *Key events in executives' lives*. Greensboro, NC: Center for Creative Leadership, 1987, 383 pages.

This technical report presents the results of data collected from interviews and open-ended surveys with 191 successful executives from six major corporations. The executives described key events in their careers—that is, things that led to lasting change in them as managers—and what they learned from these events. The resulting 616 stories and 1,547 lessons were sorted by similarity into 16 kinds of events (for example, fix-it assignments, business failures and mistakes, role models, and coursework) and 34 categories of lessons (for example, how to direct and motivate subordinates, getting lateral cooperation, and seeing organizations as systems).

The major portion of this report consists of detailed descriptions of and examples from these event and lesson categories. Appendices provide various graphs and tables that show the distribution of lessons across event categories and the significant patterns linking events and lessons. This study was the basis for the McCall, Lombardo, and Morrison 1988 book, *The Lessons of Experience*; and this report serves as a technical companion piece to that book.

Danity M. Little. *How executives learn: The demographic impact on executive development in the public service.* Doctoral dissertation, 1991, University of Southern California, Los Angeles.

This study examined the career pathways (that is, routes, learnings, and experiences) of successful Senior Executive Service (SES) career women. The same research method used in the CCL studies of executive development (McCall et al., 1988; Morrison et al., 1987) was employed with a sample of 78 SES female executives. These women described key events in their careers and what they had learned from these events.

Two common patterns of career progression were associated with successful entry into the SES: the woman had to be competent and to become noticed for her abilities, expertise, or knowledge; and she usually had a mentor who guided her, provided the right opportunities at the right time in her career, or paved the way for her success.

The two most frequently reported key events in this sample were bosses and role models, and managing a larger-scope job. Bosses and role models provided guidance, support, and opportunities. Managing a larger-scope job provided the chance for the executive to test her management skills, to take risks, to learn while coping with a myriad of situations, and to understand her own strengths and weaknesses. Other higher-frequency events included project/task force assignments, changing jobs, first supervisory jobs, starting something from scratch, early work experiences, and coursework.

Although a wide variety of lessons were reported, four stood out in the study: (1) learning all about how government works, (2) acquiring technical and professional skills, (3) learning how to handle political people and situations, and (4) developing self-confidence. A comparison of the findings between this study of public-sector women and CCL's study of women executives in the private sector revealed more similarities than differences in the experiences and lessons learned. However, the SES women were more focused on learning about the system of government and mastery of specific managerial skills than were the private-sector women. The SES women also reported more assignment-based developmental experiences than women in the private sector.

Charles Margerison and Andrew Kakabadse. *How American chief executives succeed: Implications for developing high-potential employees.* New York: American Management Association, 1984, 45 pages.

The emphasis of this study was on what CEOs do and how, in their view, they have succeeded. The research began with extensive interviews with CEOs in a variety of industries. The information collected was used to design a questionnaire to which 711 CEOs responded. They answered numerous questions about their activities as CEOs and about the key influences on their career development.

The top-rated key influences were (in rank order): a need to achieve results, the ability to work easily with a wide variety of people, challenge in their career, a willingness to take risks, early overall responsibility for important tasks, breadth of experience in many functions prior to the age of 35, a desire to seek new opportunities, and leadership experience early in their career. Role models and management training were ranked in the lower fifth of key influences.

The CEOs were also asked to name the three most important things they had to learn in order to perform their role as an executive. Communication was the most frequently mentioned activity, followed by strategic planning, managing people, delegation, patience, and decision making.

The survey also yielded information on the parts of the job CEOs experienced as most difficult, the things that take up most of their work time, how they would describe other effective executives they had known, and the management development areas that they would concentrate on in developing others for senior responsibilities in the organization.

Implications of the survey results are discussed in terms of five questions: (1) How can we tell that a young manager has executive potential? (2) What practical experience does a high-potential executive require? (3) How long should a high-potential manager stay in one job? (4) What approaches to off-the-job training hold the most promise? (5) How important is on-the-job management development?

Morgan W. McCall, Jr., Michael M. Lombardo, and Ann M. Morrison. *The lessons of experience: How successful executives develop on the job.* Lexington, MA: Lexington Books, 1988, 210 pages.

This book focuses on the kinds of experiences that contribute to the growth of successful managers. The authors interviewed 191 successful executives. These executives were asked to identify three key events that made a difference in their careers. The book focuses on what happened and what they learned from these events.

The lessons executives reported learning from their key events were categorized into five themes: (1) setting and implementing agendas—the ability to set short- and long-term goals with the flexibility to accommodate the uncertainty of organizational dynamics and time factors; (2) handling relationships—working through and with other people; (3) basic values—the appreciation of certain guiding principles such as sensitivity to human sides of management; (4) executive temperament—personal qualities necessary to be a leader, such as appropriate usage of power and self-confidence; and (5) personal awareness—adequate insight relating to one's career and personal life. The key events themselves covered three broad categories of experience: assignments, other people, and hardships. A separate chapter is dedicated to each of these categories.

The authors identified seven types of developmental assignments: first supervisory job, early work experiences, a switch from a line job to a staff job, handling a project or a task force, starting from scratch, fix-it/turnaround assignments, and increases in scope. A different pattern of lessons was associated with each type of assignment. For example, a switch from a line job to a staff job tended to teach lessons in handling relationships, such as learning how to work with executives, strategies of negotiation, and dealing with conflict.

These assignments were especially developmental because of the challenges they contained. To succeed at them, managers had to learn. The authors point out four core elements of these assignments: (1) managers found themselves in situations that required the application of skills never used before, (2) they experienced intense pressure to get things done and done right, (3) the situations often involved interpersonal conflicts that directly or indirectly interfered with the task at hand and brought forth an emphasis on managers' interpersonal skills, and (4) the assignments were usually physically and mentally exhausting.

Not all learning comes from assignments. About twenty percent of the key events featured a specific person (usually a superior) rather than an assignment and twenty percent were categorized as hardships, such as career setbacks, business failures and mistakes, and subordinate performance problems. From others, managers reported learning about management values, human values, what executives are like, and organizational politics. Hardships forced managers to face themselves and come to grips with their own fallibility.

The authors provide chapters directed toward the manager who wants to make the best of his or her experience and toward organizations who are looking for strategies for developing their managers. Their advice to managers includes the following: seek out a variety of expanding, broadening opportunities; develop the capability to be a quick study, to be an astute people watcher, and to look inside yourself and deal with your feelings and motives; have a clear sense of yourself and your shortcomings; and accept responsibility for your own development. The authors also explore four questions that organizations who are considering undertaking a serious management development program should ask: Does the organization have strong corporate identity? Is the corporation willing to take developmental risks? Is the culture of the organization supportive of learning? Is the organization willing to identify and monitor a pool of promising talent?

Ann M. Morrison, Randall P. White, and Ellen Van Velsor. *Breaking the glass ceiling: Can women reach the top of America's largest corporations?* Reading, MA: Addison-Wesley, 1992 (updated edition), 229 pages.

As part of a study of top female executives in Fortune 100-sized corporations, the authors asked seventy-six women in executive positions about key events in their careers and lessons learned from these events. Their answers were useful in addressing one of this book's key questions: How did these women get as far as they did in corporate America?

The authors found that six lessons were common to the career experiences of these women: learn the ropes, take control of your career, build confidence, rely on others, go for "the bottom line," and integrate life and work. These lessons represented developmental leaps that the women made to cope with the demands being placed on them.

Twenty-three types of key events were derived from these women's descriptions of their learning experiences. These fell within six broad categories: (1) significant job changes (first management job and move to corporate staff), (2) other people (helpful bosses and bad bosses), (3) hassles and disappointments (firing a problem employee and missing a promotion),

(4) challenging assignments (negotiations or chairing a task force), (5) getting tuned in (getting feedback and learning the ropes about corporate politics), and (6) off-the-job experiences (having children and family relocations).

In addition to looking at the experiences and lessons that enabled these women to be successful, the book also addresses the narrow band of acceptable behavior for female executives, barriers that keep women out of senior management, and how female executives might deal with these barriers.

Samuel E. Perry. *Key events in the lives of successful middle school principals in Virginia.* Doctoral dissertation, 1994, Virginia Polytechnic Institute and State University, Richmond.

Using the methodology developed by McCall, Lombardo, and Morrison (1988), the author investigated the key events in the careers of six of the most successful middle school principals in the state of Virginia. Middle school principals are responsible for managing a relatively large number of individuals and activities. Nine key event themes were identified in the interviews: new or first administrative job, personal influence, handling change, personnel problems, role models/colleague support, student success, success with parents, conferences, and divine intervention. Some of these themes overlap those found by McCall, Lombardo, and Morrison (for example, new or first administrative job and handling change) and others are more specific to the job of middle school principals (for example, student success and success with parents).

The most frequent events mentioned were new or first administrative job and personal influence, the latter referring to certain off-the-job experiences that had an impact on how they approached their work. Perry identified twenty lessons that principals derived from these developmental events (for instance, do what is best for kids, how to work with staff, be decisive, stay open to learning).

Although the interviewed principals were highly educated individuals with extensive experience in formal training programs, most if not all of their development was reported as being the direct result of on-the-job experiences or experiences with other people. With the exception of participation in conferences, experiences seemed to be the primary source of their development.

A. Rebecca Reuber and Eileen M. Fischer. The learning experiences of entrepreneurs. In *Frontiers of Entrepreneurship Research*. Proceedings of the Babson Entrepreneurship Research Conference, Houston, TX, 1993, pp. 234-245.

This paper explores the nature of the learning experiences of entrepreneurs. Entrepreneurial experience has been widely studied in order to explain why some entrepreneurial firms are more successful than others. The findings from empirical research examining the relationship between owner experience and firm performance have been mixed, partially due to inconsistencies across studies in the experience and performance measures used. The authors thus argue that a more detailed examination of what is meant by "valuable experience" is needed.

The authors surveyed over forty owners of technological firms who were responsible for starting the venture. These entrepreneurs rated how valuable thirty-three types of experiences had been in allowing them to develop the skills necessary to manage their current firm. These experiences included their education, advice received from others (such as partners, customers, and consultants), and experiences in their previous and current firm (for example, owning the firm, facing major setbacks, and supervising others). Experiences in the current and previous firm were rated as more valuable than education and advice from others. Five experiences in the current firm were rated as most valuable: owning and managing the firm, facing major successes, the process of starting the firm, facing major setbacks, and supervising managers.

The authors conclude that the most effective learning for entrepreneurs occurs when knowledge is tied to the context in which it is used. This calls into question the way that owner experience has been measured in previous studies, namely, those that measure experience previous to owning the current firm. The authors suggest that researchers need to take into account the quality of entrepreneurs' experience, not just amount of experience.

A. Rebecca Reuber and Eileen M. Fischer. Entrepreneurs' experience, expertise, and the performance of technology-based firms. *IEEE Transactions on Engineering Management*, 41:4, 1994, pp. 365-374.

This study examines the relationship between the experience of owners and the performance of their firms. It posits that the relationship between experience and performance is mediated by expertise; that is, experience produces expertise, which in turn produces enhanced performance outcomes.

This proposition is explored by testing three hypotheses: (1) Owner expertise has a stronger association with firm performance than does owner experience. (2) Different types of owner experience are associated with different types of owner expertise. (3) Owner experience has a direct relationship to firm performance in addition to an indirect relationship mediated by owner expertise.

Data to test these hypotheses were collected from owners of forty-three biotechnology and telecommunications firms. They indicated whether they had previous management, industry, small-firm, large-firm, and start-up experience. They also rated their own expertise in sixteen functional areas as well as the importance of and their satisfaction with their firm's performance on seventeen performance indicators. In addition, objective measures of firm performance were available.

The findings indicated that owner expertise is more strongly associated with firm performance than is owners' experience; that different types of expertise are associated with different types of experience; and that there is a small direct association of experience on firm performance. The linkages found between experience and expertise made intuitive sense to the authors. For example, start-up experience was significantly correlated with expertise used during the start-up process (namely, feasibility analysis, developing global operations, financial analysis, and financing). Of all the experience measures, small-firm experience had the most significant correlations with expertise. The authors argue that this is reasonable because small-firm experience requires the owner to be involved in a broad base of the firm's operations.

The authors conclude that experience measures are inadequate surrogates for expertise. Use of these surrogates is based on the assumption that all individuals learn equally from these experiences and that all experiences labeled in the same way are equally rich learning environments. They suggest that the following questions need to be closely examined: What types of experiences are most valuable? Is depth or breadth of experience more valuable? From a practice perspective, their findings suggest that expertise in certain strategic areas such as strategic planning, globalization, and strategic alliance formation are more consequential for firm performance, and thus entrepreneurs should seek experiences that help them develop expertise in these areas. They also suggest that investors and lenders should rely less on the experience of the owner and probe more for evidence of expertise when making investment decisions.

Anna Marie Valerio. A study of the developmental experiences of managers. In K. E. Clark & M. B. Clark (Eds.), *Measures of leadership*. West Orange, NJ: Leadership Library of America, 1990, pp. 521-534.

This study focuses on the developmental experiences reported by successful managers at New York Telephone. During the decentralization process that occurred at AT&T during the mid-1980s, the company set out to assess the developmental nature of different job experiences using the key-event methodology developed by McCall, Lombardo, and Morrison (1988). Forty-one middle- to upper-level managers generated 143 events that were perceived as instrumental to their growth as managers. These key events were grouped into nineteen categories, ten of which (the most frequent ones) are reported by Valerio: promotion/increase in scope, special projects, exposure to a role model, self-initiated activities, negative experiences, start-up operations, rotation to AT&T, staff person to vice president, unique positions, and attendance at assessment center. Each of these events were associated with specific lessons learned. For example, negative experiences were associated with learning the importance of effective interpersonal skills, the necessity for good follow-up, and patience and humility.

Valerio further explored the link between managerial competencies and developmental experiences by asking managers to describe which on-the-job and off-the-job events contributed to the growth of specific managerial competencies (for instance, written communications, planning, and decisiveness). The result is a list of both work and nonwork developmental experiences. For example, on-the-job experiences that contributed to behavior flexibility included responding to the needs of others and job transfer. Off-the-job experiences that contributed to the same competency were community activities, personal experiences in dealing with one's family, moving, and psychotherapy.

The results of the research are being used in a new development program for middle managers that includes an emphasis on lateral movement for development, programs for women and minority managers, and the establishment of a core curriculum for skills training.

Calhoun W. Wick. How people develop: An in-depth look. *HR Reporter*, 6:7, July 1989, pp. 1-3.

This article briefly describes findings from Wick and Company's research on career development. Managers participating in their seminars were asked to share key developmental experiences in their careers that enabled them to make the kinds of contributions they currently make to their organizations. The vast majority of the experiences described occurred on the job: 32% were transfers to new assignments, 25% were experiences within an assignment, and 17% were relationships within an assignment. Four factors characterized developmental experiences: (1) Challenge: changes that are viewed as a challenge to be conquered or an opportunity to learn new skills, (2) Novelty: opportunities to do something new, (3) Responsibility: account-ability for the success or failure of one's actions, and (4) Control: self-initiation or a sense of choice in accepting a developmental opportunity.

Ron Zemke. The Honeywell studies: How managers learn to manage. *Training,* August 1985, pp. 46-51.

This article describes a six-year research effort at Honeywell, Inc., that focused on how managers learn to manage. The first phase of the research, conducted from 1979 to 1980, found that successful Honeywell managers learn the most about managing from their job experiences and assignments. Good relationships with others and formal training and education also con-tributed to development; however, training was most effective if it occurred at or near the time of a significant transition in assignment. The second phase of research, known as The Job and Relationships Project, reexamined the relative importance of experiences, relationships, and training and examined in more depth how these factors affect management development. The second phase was more loosely sanctioned by the organization and operated more as a "skunk works" project.

Phase two results led to revisions and supplements to the conclusions from phase one. The original conclusion was that eighty percent of manage-rial learning came from job experiences; based on phase two data, the impor-tance of relationships and training was more clearly articulated, accounting for fifty percent of learning (rather than the original estimate of twenty percent). The researchers also found that relationships with subordinates and supervisors were crucial to helping a manager become competent in an assignment; that taking charge of new or struggling projects or coaching others helped develop managerial competence within an assignment (without changing jobs); that to develop subordinates managers needed to balance support and autonomy; and that key hindrances to learning were lack of time for personal development, lack of opportunity for advancement, and a boss who placed heavy emphasis on short-term results. The research suggested that in order to do a better job of developing managers, executives at Honeywell needed to articulate a philosophy of development, mandate training at certain levels, recognize the power of nontraining development opportunities, make cross-functional and cross-divisional assignments, and reward managers for developing subordinates.

Section 1.2: Development in Current Jobs

David Kelleher, Peter Finestone, and Alex Lowy. Managerial learning: First notes on an unstudied frontier. *Group and Organization Studies*, 11:3, 1986, pp. 169-202.

This study investigated how managers learn informally on the job, in response to the pressures of the environment. The authors hypothesized that job, person, and contextual variables would be related to the level of learning activity derived from day-to-day managerial experiences. The first step was to classify the forty-three managers in the study into one of three categories of learning activity (low, medium, or high). This classification was based on seven criteria, including the managers' involvement in a management development program, their supervisors' ratings of the learning activity, and the amount of learning reported in two interviews.

Differences were found between high and low learners in how they experienced their jobs. High learners reported more opportunity and pressure to learn in their jobs, were more likely to be in jobs demanding improvisation or policy development, managed more subordinates, and experienced more role ambiguity and overload.

The relationships between learning activity and two types of person variables—personal variables (orientation to people and articulation) and demographic characteristics (age and salary)—were also investigated. Orientation to people was found to be more of a concern for high learners. High learners viewed dealing with people as being a large part of their job, while low learners did not perceive this aspect of their job as very important. Another personal variable related to learning activity was "framework"; in self-reports of their managerial approaches, high learners' concept of management emphasized openness to their environment, while low learners leaned toward a more authoritarian approach. In terms of demographic characteristics, this study found gender and promotion rate to be related to learning activity. Female managers were more likely to be classified in the high learner group, as were those managers who were promoted frequently.

Learning was also found to be contingent upon organizational context. High learners were more likely to be in contexts that were characterized by freedom and encouragement to innovate, goal ambiguity, change, supervisory pressure, and opportunities to communicate.

Based on their study, the authors propose a model for understanding the managerial learning process. In the model, change or the demands of managing staff begin the learning process. If supervisory pressure and a personal orientation to learning are present, learning is likely to be precipitated. Two other factors then become important: the personal quality of openness and the level of influence needed to obtain the information, support, and latitude for learning.

Two practical implications are proposed. First, the manager's supervisor plays a very important role in the learning process. Supervisors are responsible, more than any other organizational player, in shaping the context and the job, and enabling the emergence of the personal characteristics associated with high learners. Second, the manager's understanding of the learning process through feedback should facilitate learning.

❖❖❖

Cynthia D. McCauley, Patricia J. Ohlott, and Marian N. Ruderman. On-the-job development: A conceptual model and preliminary investigation. *Journal of Managerial Issues*, 1:2, 1989, pp. 142-158.

The authors propose a framework for understanding the role of job assignments in on-the-job learning. In the model they present, job transitions and job demands are the two main precursors of on-the-job learning. Job transitions involve changes in level, organizational unit, and location or represent important first experiences. Transitions are characterized by novelty and the need to adapt. Job demands, on the other hand, are recurring aspects of a manager's job that are developmental. They include creating changes in the workplace, performing in high-stakes situations, dealing with uncertainty, and experiencing supervisor pressure. Job transitions and job demands stimulate a sense of challenge in the manager (for example, he or she feels stretched by the job). The manager reacts adaptively to the challenge by seeking information, taking action, increasing effort, trying new behaviors, or building new relationships. These adaptive reactions in turn lead to learning. Feedback, reinforcement, and support play important roles in the learning process, as does the individual's past experiences, self-esteem, learning orientation, and development needs.

A preliminary test of this model was undertaken using data collected with the Job Challenge Profile (JCP), a questionnaire that asks managers to rate their jobs in terms of various job demands and to rate the degree to which they are learning various lessons from their jobs. The content of the instrument is based on the McCall, Lombardo, and Morrison (1988) interviews with executives about the key learning events in their careers. Four linkages in the model were tested: job demands and on-the-job learning, job transitions and on-the-job learning, job demands and job transitions, and past experiences and on-the-job learning. Support for all these linkages were found.

The authors conclude that on-the-job learning can be achieved through both job transitions and recurring job demands. Furthermore, it appears that challenging assignments account for only part of the learning outcomes. Over seventy percent of the variance in learning outcomes was not accounted for by the transitions and demands that characterize a challenging assignment. The authors argue that individual differences in terms of recognizing, accepting, and learning from the challenge may account for much of this variance. The role of the organization is also mentioned in terms of providing feedback, reinforcement, and support to the developing manager.

Cynthia D. McCauley, Marian N. Ruderman, Patricia J. Ohlott, and Jane E. Morrow. Assessing the developmental components of managerial jobs. *Journal of Applied Psychology*, 79:4, 1994, pp. 544-560.

The authors describe the development of and build validity evidence for the *Developmental Challenge Profile (DCP)*, an instrument for assessing the developmental components of managerial jobs. The content of the *DCP* was based on key elements of developmental assignments as described by McCall, Lombardo, and Morrison (1988) and by Morrison, White, and Van Velsor (1987). (In previously published research, this instrument was referred to as the Job Challenge Profile or JCP.)

Using a 116-item questionnaire, 692 managers rated the degree to which various key elements were descriptive of their current job. Factor analysis of the data yielded fifteen scales which the authors grouped into five categories: (1) *Job transitions:* Unfamiliar Responsibilities and Proving Yourself; (2) *Creating change:* Developing New Directions, Inherited Problems, Reduction Decisions, and Problems with Employees; (3) *High levels of responsibility:* High Stakes, Managing Business Diversity, Job Overload, and Handling External Pressure; (4) *Nonauthority relationships:* Influencing without Authority; and (5) *Obstacles:* Adverse Business Conditions, Lack of Top Management Support, Lack of Personal Support, and Difficult Boss.

Two strategies were used to assess the validity of the scales: relating them to the respondents' assessment of their on-the-job learning and testing hypotheses about how the scales would relate to other key variables (organizational level, domestic versus foreign assignments, and task quality). Results showed that all scales, except the four obstacle scales, were related to perceptions of learning and development and that sets of scales were differentially related to other key variables in expected ways.

The authors conclude that the *DCP* has potential as a tool for furthering the study of development through job assignments and for helping managers better understand how jobs contribute to their development. They also suggest directions for further research: longitudinal research to study the outcomes of developmental assignments, research that more closely examines the role of stress and support in on-the-job learning, and investigations of individual differences that might moderate the relationship between job assignments and learning.

Alan W. Pearson and Cynthia D. McCauley. Job demands and managerial learning in the research and developmental function. *Human Resource Development Quarterly*, 2:3, 1991, pp. 263-275.

This study focuses on the job demands and learning patterns of managers in research and development (R&D) functions. The scientific and technical skills that enabled these managers to progress need, at some point, to be augmented with managerial skills in order for them to continue to progress within the organization. The authors note a few characteristics of the R&D population that distinguishes it from the general managerial population and that are likely to affect their learning process: R&D managers are more likely to have spent a lot of time in formal education, are exposed to less variance in job assignments within R&D functions, and are exposed to different feedback contingencies (delayed feedback for success of particular assignment).

The Job Challenge Profile (JCP) was administered to 85 R&D managers from the U.S. and the U.K. The results indicated that R&D managers do face many of the same developmental job challenges as other managers. In fact on a majority of the scales there were no differences between the R&D sample and a comparison sample. R&D managers did report more problems with supervisors and with subordinates in addition to a greater lack of support from top management. R&D managers also report learning less from their jobs in the areas of interpersonal competencies.

The authors suggest that R&D managers should be sensitized to the learning potential of on-the-job development, particularly in the area of interpersonal skills. Moreover, formal training programs could be coupled with on-the-job learning, given the particular affinity of this group for structured training.

Marian N. Ruderman, Patricia J. Ohlott, and Cynthia D. McCauley. Assessing opportunities for leadership development. In K. E. Clark & M. B. Clark (Eds.), *Measures of leadership.* West Orange, NJ: Leadership Library of America, 1990, pp. 547-562.

This chapter describes initial research in the development of the Job Challenge Profile (JCP; now called the *Developmental Challenge Profile*), a questionnaire for assessing sources of on-the-job development. The questionnaire asks managers to rate 155 items describing aspects of their job. The items were derived from the McCall, Lombardo, and Morrison (1988) interviews with executives in which the executives described key developmental experiences in their careers.

Data from 346 managers and executives were used to develop twelve scales that measure sources of development: Lack of Top-management Support, Supportive Boss, Lack of Strategic Direction, Conflict with Boss, Intense Pressure, Downsizing/Reorganization, Achieving Goals through Personal Influence, Problem Subordinates, Establishing Personal Credibility, Revitalizing a Unit, External Pressures, and Inherited Problems. All but four of these scales were significantly related to the managers' global assessments of the developmental level of their job. All scales were related to ratings of learning particular lessons. Different lessons were associated with different scales; for instance, learning about institutional politics was associated with having a conflict with the boss, and learning about making decisions was associated with having intense pressure in the job. Differences in sources of development between line and staff jobs and between promotions and lateral moves were also found.

Although this initial research is promising, the authors point out additional research questions that need to be addressed, including obtaining external (rather than self-) assessments of development on the job and understanding what distinguishes individuals who learn more from their jobs than others. Potential uses of the JCP are also discussed.

Section 1.3: Transitions to New Jobs or Work Roles

John E. Beck. Expatriate management development: Realizing the learning potential of the overseas assignment. In the *Proceedings of the Academy of Management 48th Annual Meeting*, 1988, pp. 112-116.

The author suggests that the learning potential of overseas assignments has not been adequately exploited. Previous studies have shown that managers who were exposed to international assignments reported increased self-confidence, a higher tolerance for ambiguity, greater empathy toward others, and the ability to take multiple perspectives in assessing a situation. The fact that these skills are highly valuable in management contribute to the potential of overseas assignment as a development tool. However, those assignments are costly in nature and their failure rate is very high. The adjustment to a new culture almost invariably leads to some decrease in efficiency and increase in stress level.

The author proposes a model of the learning process by which expatriate managers learn from their experiences. This model originated from work conducted in sensitivity training groups and also draws on Kelly's (1955) personal construct theory and Argyris and Schon's (1974) learning model. The premise of the model is that managers' expectations are likely to be disconfirmed in any new setting. The disconfirmation process is often accelerated during international assignments in which expectations about oneself and one's work change dramatically. A common reaction to the disconfirmation is a defensive one. Managers can deny the disconfirming cues that they receive from their new environment by discrediting the source of these cues. This can take the form of rationalizing one's experience and isolating oneself from the new environment. Beck states that this defensive approach can be dissolved with the help of others. The presence of someone that understands both cultures facilitates the establishment of a cultural bridge for the manager. At this point, disconfirmation stops being a problem and becomes an opportunity to develop.

Beck proposes to apply the components of Revans' Action Learning (1986) to facilitate managerial development through international assignments. The basic steps are: (1) the need for a "real project" or a tangible experience as a vehicle for development (assignment to another country constitutes a real project), (2) the establishment of a "learning set" or a group of managers who are facing similar situations, and (3) the access to an advisor or "cultural mentor" who will facilitate the transition from a defensive stance to a development one.

❖❖❖

Jeanne M. Brett. Job transitions and personal and role development. In K. M. Rowland & G. R. Ferris (Eds.), *Research in personnel and human resources management* (Vol. 2). Greenwich, CT: JAI Press, 1983, pp. 155-185.

This article explores the potential of job transitions for personal development (changes in behavior from the old job to the new job that are eventually reflected in changed abilities, values, and attitudes) and for role development (job behaviors exhibited by the new role incumbent that were not engaged in by the previous role incumbent). Rationales for why job transitions may or may not provide opportunities for development are presented. A model of factors leading to personal and/or role development is proposed.

Job transitions provide opportunities for change because they disrupt routines and tear them loose from the environment in which they were normally enacted, allowing for new behaviors to be attached to new stimuli in the new situation. On the other hand, disruption of routines is aversive and anxiety-producing. Instead of developing new behaviors in the new job situation, the incumbent may try to quickly re-create predictability by linking old behaviors to the new stimuli. The more similar the task contents and contexts of the old and new jobs, the easier it will be to end the disruption associated with job transition by reenacting old routines.

Based on the empirical and conceptual writings of several researchers in the jobs transitions area, Brett proposes a model of the factors that influence the amount of personal and role development a new job incumbent will experience. The four factors that are most closely linked to personal development and to role development are: (1) Behavior-outcome uncertainty (uncertainty about how to obtain valued outcomes in the new job); more uncertainty leads to greater role development. (2) Effort-behavior uncertainty (uncertainty about whether one can successfully execute the behaviors required to produce outcomes); more uncertainty leads to greater personal development but less role development. (3) Expectations learning (belief that the new job is an opportunity to develop new skills); higher expectations lead to greater personal development but less role development. (4) Expectations turnaround (belief that one was selected to improve upon the job performance of the predecessor); higher expectations lead to greater role development but less personal development. Numerous variables are predicted to influence these uncertainties and expectations: amount of formal and informal socialization, task and context novelty, amount of discretion in the job and the change in amount of discretion from the previous job, self-esteem, degree of social support, environmental cues, and knowledge of the prior incumbent.

Brett argues that a single job transition should not be expected to provide opportunities for both personal and role development and suggests that organizations should explore ways to chain together a series of jobs within an organization that first stretch the individual employee and then give him or her the opportunity to stretch the organization. She offers several approaches organizations might take in doing this.

Douglas T. Hall. Breaking career routines: Midcareer choice and identity development. In D. T. Hall (Ed.), *Career development in organizations*. San Francisco: Jossey-Bass, 1986, pp. 120-159.

The author describes themes in the mid-career experience, examines what triggers new learning in mid-career, and suggests ways to facilitate mid-career growth. He defines mid-career as the period during one's career after one feels established and has achieved mastery but prior to the beginning of the disengagement process. Continued development at this point is a process of stimulating new career exploration and mastery of new skills.

Major themes in the mid-career experience include a perception of constricted career opportunities, ambiguity and uncertainty about one's future career role, a sense that one is dealing with mid-career changes alone, a decrease in the influence of organizational socialization, heightened awareness of adaptability and identity as important for career effectiveness, an increased awareness of responsibility for one's own career, increased awareness of separation from old roles, a need to disrupt habitual behavior and trigger exploration, a shift in balance from work roles to personal roles, and an increased connectedness between career transitions and life-event changes.

Hall describes how various triggers in the organization, the work role, and the person can disrupt a career routine at mid-career and lead to exploration. Under the right conditions, this "routine-busting" can lead to trial activity in new areas, changes in identity, increased adaptability, and a greater sense of being in charge of one's own career. Organizational triggers include changes in technology or external forces in the environment that call for different work skills, organization climates and reward structures that emphasize growth, and settings that tolerate taking risks. Among work role triggers are new jobs, jobs that provide continual variety and increased mastery, and the availability of role models and other developmental relationships. Personal triggers include personal life changes, dissatisfaction with the status quo, and personality factors such as flexibility or motivation for advancement.

The author suggests several steps for facilitating mid-career growth: stimulate awareness of career choice and exploration, provide an environment that stresses growth (holding managers accountable for employee development, rewarding mentoring activity, and sponsoring career exploration workshops), facilitate moves to jobs that will stretch the person in important new directions, build experience enhancement into work roles (project assignments, troubleshooting experiences, and internal consulting assignments), and create a formal career-planning program.

Linda A. Hill. *Becoming a manager*. Boston: Harvard Business School Press, 1992, 331 pages.

This book recounts the experiences of nineteen new managers during their first year on the job. It describes their challenges, how they developed and changed as they struggled with the transition to a different kind of work, and the individual and organizational resources they relied on. The participants in this research project were new sales and marketing managers, fourteen men and five women. Ten were branch managers in a securities firm and nine were sales managers in a computer company. The author collected extensive data throughout the managers' first year in these positions through observations of them at work and in training programs and interviews with them, their immediate supervisors, subordinates, and peers, as well as with senior managers and human resources managers in the organization.

Two themes ran through the managers' accounts of their first year in the job. (1) Becoming a manager required a profound psychological adjustment. To make this adjustment, they had to address four developmental tasks: learning what it means to be a manager, developing interpersonal judgment, gaining self-knowledge, and coping with stress and emotion. (2) Becoming a manager was primarily a process of learning from experience. The lessons were learned as the managers confronted daily interactions and problems. They learned incrementally and gradually. The personal changes in the managers were often difficult, both intellectually and emotionally.

Sections of the book are devoted to a more in-depth look at each of the four developmental tasks of becoming a manager. A final chapter offers suggestions on how to ease the transformation from individual contributor to manager. For the new manager, this includes being aware of common pitfalls that can occur in the transition, creating a resource base to help one deal with the challenges, and undertaking periodic self-assessments of how one is doing and whether one is suited for this new type of work. For the line manager and human resources manager, this involves developing expertise at selecting candidates for managerial positions, supporting the new manager, and developing training programs that meet the needs of the new manager (to a greater degree than most current programs).

Nigel Nicholson and Michael A. West. *Managerial job change: Men and women in transition.* Cambridge, England: Cambridge University Press, 1988, 274 pages.

This book examines work-role transitions among middle to senior managers: how much job change is taking place, who is most affected, and what the psychological consequences are for the individual manager. It is based on a large-scale study of the causes, forms, and outcomes of job change. Survey data were collected from 2,300 members of the British Institute of Management; 1,100 of these managers responded to a second survey one year later.

In the initial survey, managers described their last five job moves. After looking at the patterns in these moves, the authors concluded that most managers can expect to change jobs at least once every three years. A majority of job changes means a change of job function (not usually minor sideways steps, but a move from one family of job titles into another). Over half of all job change is "spiraling," meaning that the change results in simultaneous functional and upward status changes. In about half of these cases, spiraling takes managers out of their companies to new employers. Conventional upward career paths seem to bring the most contentment, whereas more radical and self-directed career patterns elicit more mixed sentiments.

The causes of job changes were also examined and fell into three broad types of forces: circumstantial, avoidance, and future-oriented. Most managers explain their job changes as future-oriented, that is, positive moves toward desired futures. A much smaller number were primarily avoidance moves, done to escape undesired circumstances, or circumstantial. However, if primary and secondary reasons for the move are included, for most managers a single job change springs from both future-oriented and either circumstantial or avoidance reasons.

The longitudinal nature of the study also allowed for the examination of the effects of job changes that occurred between administrations of the survey. Managers who had experienced mobility reported more personal change, particularly those with changes in status and changes in employer. Self-concept and work-preference measures taken at the time of the first and second surveys also showed some modest changes associated with particular types of job moves. For example, there was an increase in adjustment scores for those who experienced a change in employer and an increase in need for growth for those who experienced an outward spiral (change in function and status). Looking at the change data as a whole, the authors suggest that people's view of what sort of person they are is subject to change through the adjustment process brought on by a job change, while attitudinal orientations are more deeply rooted in stable individual differences.

The book also has chapters that look specifically at job moves into a newly created position and at differences between men and women in their sample. The authors conclude with implications for theory and practice in the areas of lifespan development, careers, industrial/organizational psychology, and the study of organizations and management.

Connections

Mastering a New Job

Because it is not uncommon for managers to experience new jobs every two-to-three years, there has been considerable interest in the topic of how managers master their new assignments. They must, first, understand what is expected of them in the new role and what the particular issues and problems of the new assignment are, and second, feel comfortable that they have met those expectations and dealt with the problems. Learning during this "taking charge" period is a critical part of achieving mastery. However, studies of job mastery tend to examine learning that is specific to the situation—developing an understanding of the new context and of the dynamics of the problems being worked on—rather than on developing new skills, broadening managerial competencies, or changing fundamental perspectives. There are likely connections between learning a new job and management development in the broader sense, though. Studies that explicitly bring together both perspectives are needed.

John J. Gabarro. *The dynamics of taking charge*. Boston, MA: Harvard Business School Press, 1987, 204 pages.

Meryl Reis Louis. Surprise and sense making: What newcomers experience in entering unfamiliar organizational settings. *Administrative Science Quarterly*, 25:2, 1980, pp. 226-250.

Robert F. Morrison and Thomas M. Brantner. What enhances or inhibits learning a new job? A basic career issue. *Journal of Applied Psychology*, 77:6, 1992, pp. 926-940.

Cheryl Ostroff and Steve W. J. Kozlowski. Organizational socialization as a learning process: The role of information acquisition. *Personnel Psychology*, 45:4, 1992, pp. 849-874.

Craig C. Pinder and Klaus G. Schroeder. Time to proficiency following job transfers. *Academy of Management Journal*, 30:2, 1987, pp. 336-353.

AT&T Longitudinal Studies of Managers

Researchers have been following the progress of a group of managers who were first employed by AT&T in the 1950s in a project known as the Management Progress Study. At various intervals, data have been collected on the managers' skills and abilities, lifestyles, work interests, personalities, and motivations. The impact of aging and career advancement on these factors has been examined, as well as how assessments made early in a manager's career predict later career progress and personal adjustment. In the 1970s a similar longitudinal study known as the Management Continuity Study began, which allowed for the comparison of managers who are influenced by different times. This comprehensive effort has allowed the researchers to carefully examine questions of continuity and change in adult development, advancing age versus changing times as causal factors of change, determinants of career progression, and demographic group differences.

Of particular interest to the topic of developmental assignments are results that link job challenge and career progression. Jobs high in challenge were characterized by job stimulation, supervisory responsibilities, unstructured assignments, and bosses who were achievement models. Overall ratings of job challenge in the first seven years as a manager showed a strong relationship with advancement in the organization. Also of interest is the finding that those who had reached the highest management levels at the twenty-year point in their careers had had more job changes that were across departments and locations.

Douglas W. Bray, Richard J. Campbell, and Donald L. Grant. *Formative years in business: A long-term AT&T study of managerial lives*. New York: Wiley, 1974, 236 pages.

Douglas W. Bray and Ann Howard. The AT&T longitudinal studies of managers. In K. W. Shaie (Ed.), *Longitudinal studies of adult psychological development*. New York: Guilford Press, 1983, pp. 266-312.

Ann Howard and Douglas W. Bray. *Managerial lives in transition: Advancing age and changing times*. New York: Guilford Press, 1988, 462 pages.

Tacit Knowledge

A distinction is sometimes made between academic and practical intelligence. Academic intelligence is directed toward solving problems in a school setting; these problems are generally formulated by others, have all the needed information available for solving them, and are disconnected from an individual's ordinary experience. Practical intelligence is directed toward solving problems encountered in one's life; such problems are generally unformulated, lacking all the information needed for solving them, and are related to everyday life.

Sternberg and his colleagues (1995) have advanced the notion of tacit knowledge as central to practical intelligence. Tacit knowledge is practical, action-oriented knowledge acquired through experience. It has three basic characteristics. First, it is procedural in nature in that it takes the form of "knowing how" rather than "knowing that." Second, it is practically useful in that it is instrumental to the attainment of goals people value. Third, it is usually acquired on one's own without direct help from others. Measures of tacit knowledge predict real-world criteria (such as job performance) above what is obtained from traditional cognitive ability tests.

One area that these researchers have focused on is the tacit knowledge developed by managers. These studies do support the notion that, in order to be successful, managers need to develop practical knowledge through their experiences. This includes intrapersonal knowledge, interpersonal knowledge, and organizational knowledge. Although they have not looked closely at how managers acquire tacit knowledge, recent studies have suggested that the content focus and complexity of the tacit knowledge developed by a manager is influenced by the types of challenges faced at his or her job level.

Joseph A. Horvath, George B. Forsythe, Patrick J. Sweeney, Jeffrey A. McNally, John Wattendorf, Wendy M. Williams, and Robert J. Sternberg. *Tacit knowledge in military leadership: Evidence from officer interviews* (Technical Report 1018). Alexandria, VA: U.S. Army Research Institute for the Behavioral and Social Sciences, 1994, 47 pages.

Robert J. Sternberg. *Beyond IQ: A triarchic theory of human intelligence.* New York: Cambridge University Press, 1985, 411 pages.

Robert J. Sternberg, Richard K. Wagner, Wendy M. Williams, and Joseph A. Horvath. Testing common sense. *American Psychologist*, 50:11, 1995, pp. 912-927.

Richard K. Wagner. Tacit knowledge in everyday intelligent behavior. *Journal of Personality and Social Psychology*, 52:6, 1987, pp. 1236-1247.

Richard K. Wagner and Robert J. Sternberg. Practical intelligence in real-world pursuits: The role of tacit knowledge. *Journal of Personality and Social Psychology*, 49:2, 1985, pp. 436-458.

Richard K. Wagner and Robert J. Sternberg. Tacit knowledge and intelligence in the everyday world. In R. J. Sternberg & R. K. Wagner (Eds.), *Practical intelligence: Nature and origins of competence in the everyday world*. New York: Cambridge University Press, 1986, pp. 51-83.

Richard K. Wagner and Robert J. Sternberg. Street smarts. In K. E. Clark & M. B. Clark (Eds.), *Measures of leadership*. West Orange, NJ: Leadership Library of America, 1990, pp. 493-504.

Work as a Context for Adult Development

Michael Basseches (1984) has pointed out that although studies of adult development have sometimes considered the effects of major work events on development, the effects on development of the kinds of jobs an individual holds has for the most part been neglected. At the same time, psychologists who have focused on the workplace have rarely included concepts from adult development in their work. More recent work in adult development has examined how the demands of individuals' jobs or organizational contexts are related to their level of cognitive, moral, and interpersonal development. For example, Rulon (in Demick & Miller, 1993) looks at the relationship between job complexity and workers' moral development. Kegan (1994) argues that organizations are putting more demands on workers to be self-initiating, to take responsibility for what happens to them, and to see the organization as a whole, and that these demands call for a qualitatively different order of mental complexity.

Basseches, in his work on cognitive development in adults, has most clearly emphasized the importance of challenges in the work setting for the development of more complex ways of thinking—what he refers to as dialectical thinking. Dialectical thinking emphasizes change, wholeness, and internal relations and has the power to deal with relationships and transformations beyond that possible with formal analysis. Basseches identified three work-setting challenges that are natural stimulants for the development of dialectical thinking: (1) adapting the organization to changing circumstances, (2) improving the organization's relationships with customers and suppliers, and (3) improving the coordination of activities within the organization. In most current organizations, the potential for involvement with these challenges increases at higher organizational levels; thus the potential for cognitive development increases with higher levels of responsibility.

Michael Basseches. *Dialectical thinking and adult development.* Norwood, NJ: Ablex Publishing, 1984, 420 pages.

Jack Demick and Patrice M. Miller (Eds.). *Development in the workplace.* Hillsdale, NJ: Lawrence Erlbaum, 1993, 251 pages.

Robert Kegan. *In over our heads: The mental demands of modern life.* Cambridge, MA: Harvard University Press, 1994, 396 pages.

Melvin L. Kohn and Carmi Schooler. Job conditions and personality: A longitudinal assessment of their reciprocal effects. *American Journal of Sociology,* 87:6, 1982, pp. 1257-1283.

Melvin L. Kohn and Carmi Schooler. *Work and personality: An inquiry into the impact of social stratification.* Norwood, NJ: Ablex, 1983, 389 pages.

Dorothy Rulon. Significance of job complexity in workers' moral development. In J. Demick & P. M. Miller (Eds.), *Development in the workplace.* Hillsdale, NJ: Erlbaum, 1993, pp. 39-53.

William R. Torbert. *Managing the corporate dream: Restructuring for long-term success.* Homewood, IL: Dow Jones-Irwin, 1987, 250 pages.

Employee Participation in Learning and Development Activities

The perceived importance (for organizational success) of continuous learning among employees has stimulated interest in understanding the factors that motivate employees to engage in development activities. Most of this interest has been focused on professional employees, especially those in areas where knowledge is growing rapidly and thus it is easy for skills to become outdated. Most of the interest has also focused on employee engagement in formal development activities such as training programs, college courses, reading, and conference attendance; however, some of the work has extended to include on-the-job development activities.

Research in this area has examined the role of job challenge as both a means and a motivator of continuous learning (Pazy, 1996). That is, jobs that provide novelty, breadth, responsibility, interaction with others who have different approaches, completion of projects from beginning to end, and feedback from others are a source of learning. And they also provide a motivation to learn and to seek out other development activities because they point out gaps in the employee's current level of competence. More recently, research in this area has begun to look at individual differences in motivation to pursue learning and development opportunities (Maurer & Tarulli, 1994; Noe & Wilk, 1993) and at the individual's understanding of and affective response to perceived lack of knowledge to do one's job adequately (Pazy, 1995, 1996).

Samuel S. Dubin. Maintaining competence through updating. In S. L. Willis & S. S. Dubin (Eds.), *Maintaining professional competence*. San Francisco: Jossey-Bass, 1990, pp. 9-43.

James L. Farr and Carolyn L. Middlebrooks. Enhancing motivation to participate in professional development. In S. L. Willis & S. S. Dubin (Eds.), *Maintaining professional competence*. San Francisco: Jossey-Bass, 1990, pp. 195-213.

Steve W. J. Kozlowski and James L. Farr. An integrative model of updating and performance. *Human Performance*, 1:1, 1988, pp. 5-29.

Steve W. J. Kozlowski and Brian M. Hults. An exploration of climates for technical updating and performance. *Personnel Psychology*, 40:3, 1987, pp. 539-563.

Todd J. Maurer and Beverly A. Tarulli. Investigation of perceived environment, perceived outcome, and person variables in relationship to voluntary development activity by employees. *Journal of Applied Psychology*, 79:1, 1994, pp. 3-14.

Donald Britton Miller. Organizational, environmental, and work design strategies that foster competence. In S. L. Willis & S. S. Dubin (Eds.), *Maintaining professional competence*. San Francisco: Jossey-Bass, 1990, pp. 233-248.

Raymond A. Noe and Steffanie L. Wilk. Investigation of the factors that influence employees' participation in development activities. *Journal of Applied Psychology*, 78:2, 1993, pp. 291-302.

Asya Pazy. Professionals' experience of lack of knowledge: A phenomenological study. *Journal of Social Behavior and Personality*, 10:4, 1995, pp. 907-922.

Asya Pazy. Concept and career-stage differentiation in obsolescence research. *Journal of Organizational Behavior*, 17:1, 1996, pp. 59-78.

SECTION 2: INDIVIDUAL VARIABILITY IN ON-THE-JOB DEVELOPMENT

Overview

This section contains annotations of articles and books that speak to differences in how individuals learn from job experiences. In particular we look at learning styles, ability to learn from experience, and the impact of demographic variables on learning from experience. The research findings are organized around three key conclusions: (1) different people approach learning from their experiences in different ways, (2) some people are particularly adept at learning from job experiences, and (3) gender and other demographic variables have impact on developmental assignments.

In general, there is less systematic research on the role of individual differences in on-the-job development than there is on the kinds of experiences that are developmental for managers. Thus, although there is some support for these general conclusions, the specific research findings are more tenuous than those in the previous section.

Various learning theorists have used some version of a cyclical learning model to describe the process of learning from experience. At its simplest, this learning model posits that individuals take action based on their current knowledge and mental frameworks for understanding a situation, observe and reflect on the consequences of their actions, and then revise their understanding based on these observations and consequences. Then the cycle is repeated. The experiential learning cycle holds promise as a model for integrating research on individual differences in on-the-job learning. Thus, when we address research directions, we return to the concept of a learning cycle and provide an overview and list of references on this topic in the "Connections" section.

Individual differences in motivation and ability to learn have also been studied by educators who are interested in how individuals can learn more effectively in educational settings and how the educational system can better prepare individuals for lifelong learning. Although the learning context in much of this work is more formal than that for on-the-job learning, some of it has been extended to include learning outside of the classroom. We have included an overview of this area, often referred to as *learning to learn*, in the "Connections" section.

Key Findings and Implications

Different people approach learning from their experiences in different ways.

Those who have looked at how people approach the task of learning have tended to frame these approaches as either learning styles or learning strategies. These two frames often overlap. However, when the frame is learning styles, there tends to be a greater emphasis on typologies of individuals based on their style and on the styles being reflective of broad personal orientations or preferences. A strategies frame puts more emphasis on what individuals actually do as they try to learn (rather than on broad orientations toward learning) and, although this frame recognizes that there are clusters of strategies that are used more frequently by some people than others, it puts less emphasis on categorizing people into learning types.

The best-known research and theory on learning styles is that of David Kolb (1984). Two basic assumptions underlie his work: People learn from immediate, here-and-now experience, and people learn differently; that is, according to their preferred learning styles. He delineates four primary learning styles: convergent, divergent, assimilative, and accommodative. These styles can be differentiated in terms of two processes central to learning: how experience is grasped (through concrete experience or abstract conceptualization) and how experience is transformed into knowledge (by active experimentation or reflective observation).

The convergent style emphasizes abstract conceptualization and active experimentation and is thus suited to situations where there is a single best solution. On the other hand, the divergent style emphasizes concrete experience and reflective observation and is best suited to situations that call for the generation of alternative ideas. The assimilative style focuses on abstract conceptualization and reflective observation; its strength lies in assimilating disparate observations into an integrated explanation. Finally, the accommodative style is dominated by concrete experience and active experimentation, and its strength is in adapting to changing immediate circumstances. Kolb's experiential learning theory posits that all four styles are important to learning from experience but that personalities, education, career choices, and current situations shape individuals so that they tend to rely heavily on one style. Part of an individual's development task is to learn to use all the styles in an integrative fashion.

Experiential learning theory has generated considerable research. A recent search of the *Social Science Citation Index* yielded 292 articles that reference Kolb's book that summarizes his theory (Kolb, 1984). The theory has also been further developed and popularized by Honey and Mumford (1989). Some of the research on learning styles and practitioners' experience in applying the learning style model supports the theory and some raises considerable questions about it. It is beyond the scope of this bibliography to review this entire body of research. A selected reading of the literature suggests that questions about the validity of the theory focus primarily on (1) incompatibilities between the process and style view of learning (Does learning from experience unfold in a four-stage process represented by the learning cycle or does it unfold as a stylistic way of apprehending and transforming knowledge?) and (2) inadequacies in the operationalization of learning styles through self-assessment instruments.

In terms of the second issue, Kolb's instrument for measuring learning styles, the *Learning Style Inventory*, has been closely scrutinized, and at least two alternatives have been created by others (see Allinson & Hayes, 1988; Romero, Tepper, & Tetrault, 1992). Several articles related to these conceptual and measurement issues are included in the annotations, but we have by no means covered all the relevant literature.

Closely related to the notion of learning styles is the idea that managers differ in their preferences for certain types of learning strategies or approaches (Akin, 1987; Bunker & Webb, 1992; Mumford, 1995). For example, some managers might prefer to watch and emulate a role model, others might prefer to ask experts and read the literature before taking action, and still others might prefer to begin experimenting immediately. Some engage in learning by examining past experiences, and others are more planful in their approach to learning from upcoming events. As with the learning styles research, these models assume that individuals develop preferences for particular sets of learning tactics and that to maximize their effectiveness as learners, they need to become proficient at multiple tactics.

There are two main implications of research on differences in learning styles or strategies: (1) Certain learning styles may be more effective in certain developmental assignments than in others. For example, active experimentation may be more effective in turnaround assignments, whereas a more reflective style may be needed in a staff assignment. Thus, learning-style preferences may need to be considered when placing a manager in a developmental assignment. If there is a learning style-situation mismatch, extra coaching and support for the manager may be required. (2) A manager's preference for certain approaches to learning may narrow his or her learning potential. Managers need to become versatile in using multiple approaches.

Some people are particularly adept at learning from job experiences.

Research on learning styles or strategies has not tended to differentiate individuals who are skilled at learning from experience from those who are not. Styles are viewed as different approaches, with one style not being necessarily better than others. The only way that levels of learning is addressed is through assumptions that the ability to utilize multiple styles is better than having one dominant style.

Other researchers have looked more specifically at the characteristics of managers who are particularly good learners (Brett, 1983; Bunker & Webb, 1992; Dechant, 1990; Kelleher et al., 1986; Marsick & Watkins, 1990; McCall, 1994; Perkins, 1994; Ruderman, Ohlott, & McCauley, 1996; Spreitzer, McCall, & Mahoney, 1997). The factor that this research focuses on is sometimes referred to as the *ability to learn from experience*—although characteristics that appear to affect motivation to learn more directly than ability to learn are often included, too. The settings and frameworks used in the various studies are quite diverse, but several themes do emerge in descriptions of managers who are more likely to learn from job experiences:

1. *Learning orientation* (Bunker & Webb, 1992; Kelleher et al., 1986; Kotter, 1995; McCall, 1994; Perkins, 1994; Spreitzer et al., 1997). Learning is a central concept in these managers' approach to their work. They see life as a series of ongoing learning experiences. They accept responsibility for learning and seek experiences that will enhance their personal development.

2. *Proactive stance toward problems and opportunities* (Bunker & Webb, 1992; Dechant, 1990; Marsick & Watkins, 1990; McCall, 1994). These managers tackle problems head-on; they are biased toward action. They also have a sense of adventure; they like to experience new things, try out new ideas, and meet new people. When they find themselves in a new situation or identify a learning deficit in themselves, they take initiative and are very self-directed in their efforts to satisfy their learning needs.

3. *Critical reflection* (Bunker & Webb, 1992; Daudelin, 1996; Dechant, 1990; Kelleher et al., 1986; Marsick & Watkins, 1990; McCall, 1994; Perkins, 1992; Spreitzer et al., 1997). Marsick and Watkins define critical reflection as "bringing one's assumptions, premises, criteria, and schemata into consciousness and vigorously critiquing them" (p. 29). There are various ways in which these individuals engage in critical reflection. They pay attention to surprising results and try to understand them. They explore how things work, why things are the way they are, and what makes people tick. They see patterns and connections between seemingly unconnected variables. They ask lots of probing questions and look at questions from different

angles. They seek out feedback, comparison points, benchmarks, and role models. They try to understand their own strengths and weaknesses and diagnose the gaps between their current skills and what is needed in a situation.

④ *Openness* (Bunker & Webb, 1992; Kelleher et al., 1986; McCall, 1994; Spreitzer et al., 1997). Managers who appear to learn the most from their experiences are not dogmatic or autocratic. They are open to other points of view, to feedback and criticism from others, and to shifting their strategies midstream. They more readily give up ideas or behaviors that prove to be less effective. Their rules-of-thumb for managing emphasize being open to information from the environment. They are sensitive to cultural differences and change behavior in response to these differences.

Other personal characteristics that are potentially important to learning from job experiences have been found in only one study. Kelleher et al. (1986) emphasized "orientation to people"; they found active learners were more concerned with the people-management aspects of their jobs. Bunker and Webb (1992) identified several characteristics that indicated that effective learners had a positive orientation to demanding situations. They saw these situations as opportunities rather than threats, they focused on the positive implications of stressful events, and they accepted what they couldn't change about a situation and worked with it. Marsick and Watkins (1990) emphasized creativity; they concluded that people who were imaginative and able to think beyond the point of view they normally used were better able to break out of preconceived patterns. Perkins (1992) reported on research indicating that learning-oriented managers readily used metaphors and analogies and conducted discussions in a nonlinear manner. Ruderman et al. (1996) found that managers with higher self-esteem reported learning more from their jobs than did managers with lower self-esteem. Self-esteem may be a basic factor that underlies some of the other personal characteristics such as openness and positive orientation to demanding situations.

Research that points out how some people are more adept at on-the-job learning than others implies that learning from developmental assignments is not automatic. For management development to occur, organizations must not only provide assignments that stretch their managers, but must either select for or develop learning capacities in the managers and create climates where these capacities can be put to use.

McCall (1994) points out another implication of this research. If key learning-ability factors can be identified, early selection of high-potential managers should be based on these factors because the combination of learning ability and variety of developmental assignments will yield the competencies found in successful executives. This approach overcomes the problems encountered in trying to select high-potential managers early in their careers based on the competencies found in successful executives. Such competencies are unlikely to be found in managers early in their careers because they haven't had the opportunity to develop them.

Demographic variables have an impact on developmental assignments.
    Of the various demographic variables that may affect developmental assignments, gender has received the most attention. Two related factors have stimulated research focused on gender: (1) The samples in initial studies of critical experiences in managerial careers reflected the demographics of successful executives at the time; that is, these samples were primarily male. The practice of generalizing results from studies of men to women is, of course, highly suspect. Thus, replicating these studies with samples of women was necessary in order to capture the experiences of a broader population. (2) The possibility that women did not have the same access to developmental opportunities was one explanation for why more women were not making it to the senior-management ranks of organizations. Thus, data supporting this proposition would clarify the disparity and offer a strategy for getting more women into top-management positions, namely by providing them with the developmental assignments to which men have traditionally had access.

    These two factors led to the following questions that consider the impact of gender on developmental assignments: (1) Do men and women perceive developmental experiences differently? (Do they see the same experiences as developmental? Do they learn the same things? Does being a nontraditional manager change the experience and lessons for women?) (2) Do women have access to the same developmental assignments as men do? The Morrison, White, and Van Velsor (1987) study and the more direct comparison of that study's results with data from male managers (Van Velsor & Hughes, 1990) was driven more by the first question (although it also provided insights about the second question). Research by Cianni and Romberger (1995), by Ohlott, Ruderman, and McCauley (1994), and by Lyness and Thompson (1997) focused more on the second question.

    The limited research does suggest that there are gender differences in developmental experiences. Many of these differences are attributed to women being nontraditional managers in male-dominated hierarchies. For example, being the first woman to reach a particular organizational level or hold a certain position is a unique type of developmental experience for women. It creates both added challenge and added burdens; thus, it holds pluses and minuses as a developmental experience. But it does create a different type of experience for women. Another example is the types of lessons women report learning from their experiences. Van Velsor and Hughes (1990) reported that women more frequently report learning about themselves and how they fit into the organization, whereas men report more learning of new skills directly related to job performance. They argue that the more complex organizational environment faced by women stimulates more introspective learnings for them. Also, Nicholson and West (1988), in their study of job changes, noted that men were more likely to make upward moves within an organization, whereas women were more likely to change employers as they made job moves. They argue that this trend for women is at least partially due to their higher uncertainty surrounding mobility opportunities within a single organization.

Horgan (1989) argues that cognitive learning theory is a useful framework for understanding why learning from experience is different (and more difficult) for the woman manager who finds herself in a male-dominated world. Because so much of managerial work is social, and social systems are different for men and women, women face more ambiguous and complex situations. It is more difficult to extract useful rules-of-thumb or get accurate feedback in these situations.

Other differences in developmental experiences are assumed to be linked to general differences between men and women. For example, more women than men report learning from significant role models in the workplace. Although this may be partly due to women having access to fewer challenging assignments (and thus rely on other people as a primary source of learning), other studies of women would tend to support the idea that women are more attuned to learning from others. There is also some evidence that women who are attracted to managerial careers express a greater need than men for jobs that are challenging and for work that provides opportunities to learn and grow (Howard & Bray, 1988; Nicholson & West, 1988).

Additionally, there is evidence that women do not yet have equal access to all types of developmental assignments. However, the trend appears to be moving toward more equal access. Differences that remain are in the areas of high levels of responsibility and authority (for example, jobs that have high visibility, involve making critical decisions, and require integrating across business units or working with external groups) and access to important information and resource networks. Research on women in the public sector (Little, 1991) also suggests that there may be fewer access barriers in that sector. The frequencies with which various types of developmental assignments were reported by these women were close to the frequencies reported by men in corporate settings.

Research looking at other demographic variables is even more scarce than that for gender differences. We only uncovered one study that looked at race and ethnicity as a factor in on-the-job development opportunities (although we know of another study underway) and one that examined age as a factor. Although these studies do suggest that race and age are important demographic variables to continue pursuing, it would be premature to draw conclusions from them. Reasons for needing studies that focus on race and ethnicity in particular parallel those that stimulated gender studies: to broaden our understanding of the developmental experiences of an underrepresented population of managers and to examine differential access to developmental assignments.

There are two main implications of research on demographic differences in developmental assignments. (1) Organizations need to monitor the degree to which nontraditional managers have access to developmental assignments. Lack of access to developmental assignments is probably a factor contributing to fewer women and people of color making it into top-management ranks. (2) The same job may be experienced differently by a traditional and nontraditional manager. There may be additional challenges placed on the nontraditional manager, making support and rewards for development particularly important.

Research Directions

More research is needed on individual variability in on-the-job learning. Although the program of research generated by Kolb (1984) and his colleagues on learning styles is extensive, how these or other learning styles might affect the degree to which learning occurs in developmental assignments has not been closely examined. Research on ability to learn from experience has been scattered and seems to have only scratched the surface of this construct. And as noted earlier, further research on demographic variables is needed. This research should not only address questions pertaining to how people with different background vary in how they learn from experience, but also focus on variations in opportunities to experience developmental assignments. In addition, the focus on the impact of demographics on developmental experiences should be extended to include cultural differences.

Most of the research on the learning capacity of managers has not addressed whether this capacity can be enhanced over time. Kolb suggests that it can, whereas McCall (1994) suggests that it can be identified in managers early in their careers (implying that it may be more stable over time). Also, it is unclear what kind of interventions might help managers become better at learning from developmental assignments and whether these interventions would be directed at improving some ability in the individual or some aspect of the learning culture or climate in the organization. Just as we noted in Section 1, more longitudinal research is needed to address these questions.

Perhaps what is needed most in this area is an overarching theory that would help explain why managers with particular preferences, personalities, abilities, and demographic characteristics are more likely to learn from developmental assignments than others. Only Kolb provides an integrated model of experiential learning that is linked to broader learning theories. His use of the experiential learning cycle suggests that some version of this process model of learning might prove useful as a tool for integrating research on individual variability in on-the-job development. Such a model would direct researchers toward investigating personal characteristics, abilities, or behaviors that increase the likelihood that managers will seek out or be given new job experiences, take action in those assignments, observe and reflect on these actions and their consequences, and revise their understandings based on their experiences.

Annotations

Section 2.1: Learning Styles and Strategies

Gib Akin. Varieties of managerial learning. *Organizational Dynamics*, 16:2, 1987, pp. 36-48.

Akin argues that what is missing from learning models is an under-standing of the actual learning experiences of managers. To begin filling this void, he interviewed sixty managers who were seasoned veterans in various fields. He asked them to reflect on which skills, knowledge, or attitudes had been most important for achieving their success and how these determinants of managerial success had been learned.

The skills, knowledge, and attitudes that managers reported as impor-tant could be divided into six categories: interpersonal skills, analytical skills, communication skills, job knowledge, knowledge of organizational and professional norms, and self-confidence. The variety of actual learning experiences reported by the managers was large. These experiences also had different meanings for different people.

Akin noted that the managers seemed to have general frameworks that they used to organize, understand, and pursue learning activities; he labeled these "learning themes." Seven of these were identified. (1) Emulation of a mentor: the central activity in this theme is finding out as much as possible about how a recognized mentor thinks and does things and then practice those methods in real situations. (2) Role taking: the learner has a broad conception of what a competent person in their role should be, and he or she focuses on adopting the skills and attitudes specified by this role model. (3) Practical accomplishment: managers learn through the experiences of meeting chal-lenges; the guides to their learning are the outcomes of actions taken to solve problems and the feedback from other people who verify their accomplish-ments. (4) Validation: the experience of learning occurs long after the initial learning activities; it is based on authoritative information, from either a specific person or a professional source, and reinforces people's beliefs that what they have been doing all along is right. (5) Anticipation: anticipatory learners focus on learning concepts and models to use in taking action and then apply them to their practical experience. (6) Personal growth: these learners value self-understanding and personal fulfillment; they organize learning activities around self-development more than around practical accomplishments. (7) Scientific learning: the preferred pattern is to observe, conceptualize about the observations, and then experiment to collect new data.

Akin also noted that the learning process invariably started with one or both of two conditions. The need to know is one prelearning condition. The need to know is associated with a variety of experiences, such as encountering poor practice, problems that demand solutions, questions that have no answers, or personal failure. Sense of role is the other prelearning condition. This refers to a person's perception of the gap between what he or she is and what he or she should be. It results from a comparison of current skills and knowledge with those that characterize an ideal role model.

The author suggests that the information and themes his research has generated will be useful for building more learning experiences into organizational life, for tailoring developmental experiences to the needs of the learner, and for helping managers encourage and support learning in their subordinates.

❖❖❖

Christopher W. Allinson and John Hayes. The *Learning Styles Questionnaire*: An alternative to Kolb's inventory? *Journal of Management Studies*, 25:3, 1988, pp. 269-281.

This article contrasts two measures of learning styles, the *Learning Styles Questionnaire (LSQ)* and the *Learning Style Inventory (LSI)*, in terms of their practicality, psychometric qualities, and overall utility for management development programs. The *LSI* was developed by Kolb (1984) and is based on his theory of experiential learning. The authors point out concerns that have been raised about several aspects of the instrument and argue that these concerns have been addressed, at least in part, by the introduction of the *LSQ* by Honey and Mumford (1989).

Kolb's experiential learning framework and its four-stage cycle (concrete experience, reflective observation, abstract conceptualization, and active experimentation) are the theoretical basis of the *LSI*. The *LSI* uses a self-description methodology to assess the learning style of individuals. It is made up of nine sets of four words; respondents rank the words within each set according to how well they characterize their learning orientation. The instrument has been the focus of numerous reliability and validity studies. The main criticisms of the *LSI* have focused on validity of the different learning-style scales and its moderate acceptance by managerial populations.

Although Honey and Mumford's instrument, the *LSQ,* categorizes individuals along the four phases of the learning cycle, it does so with behaviorally based items (for example, "I regularly question people about their basic assumptions"). Respondents indicate the degree to which they agree or disagree with each item. An effort was also made to use labels and definitions that were meaningful to managerial populations.

The authors assessed the psychometric qualities of the *LSQ* by administering the instrument to forty managers from different countries on three separate occasions. Results from these repeated administrations indicate some stability in the factor structure of the *LSQ* across samples, a more normal distribution of scores, and relatively higher reliability coefficients and stability over time than the *LSI*. The authors note, accordingly, that this study provides only partial evidence of utility for the *LSQ* and that additional evidence is needed.

Jim Caple and Paul Martin. Reflections of two pragmatists: A critique of Honey and Mumford's learning styles. *Industrial and Commercial Training*, 26:1, 1994, pp. 16-20.

Although the authors have found Honey and Mumford's (1989) work on learning styles useful as a stimulus for understanding individual differences in ways of learning and applying that understanding to the design of training programs, their experiences have led them to question the coherence and validity of aspects of the model.

At the core of Honey and Mumford's theory is the assumption that effective learning from experience requires movement through the entire learning cycle—that is, having an experience, reviewing it, drawing conclusions from it, and taking action based on the conclusions—and that learning is deterred because people are generally better at certain stages of the cycle to the exclusion of other stages. The *Learning Styles Questionnaire* allows for the identification of learning-style preferences and helps individuals create action plans to improve weaknesses or design learning situations that take advantage of the preferred style.

The authors raise five questions about the model: (1) What is meant precisely by "experience"? (2) How accurate is the learning cycle in describing how people actually learn from experience? (3) To what extent do situational features and abilities determine the appropriateness of learning styles? (4) How realistic and meaningful are the learning style preferences? (5) How valid is the *Learning Styles Questionnaire*? In reflecting on these questions, they suggest that an improved model of learning from experience would focus on incorporating experience into the learning cycle (rather than focusing on experience as the driver of learning), delineate which forms of experience are more useful to learn from and what might be learned from them, be clearer about what is meant by "learning style," and measure learning preferences with direct questions about an individual's experience of learning (rather than using an instrument that resembles a personality questionnaire).

A response to the Caple and Martin article appeared in the same issue:

Alan Mumford. Reflections of two pragmatists: A response. *Industrial and Commercial Training*, 26:1, 1994, pp. 21-22.

Mumford addresses some of the concerns raised by Caple and Martin. He explains what he and Honey mean by "experience" and how they see the learner engaging in the learning cycle. He also refers to an earlier article and the latest *Learning Styles Questionnaire (LSQ)* manual for an explanation of why they look at general behavioral tendencies rather than directly at learning. Finally, he offers his own experiences—which appear to be different from those of Caple and Martin—in using the *LSQ*. As trainers, he and Honey often use direct questions about learning (as suggested by Caple and Martin) in conjunction with the *LSQ*.

Steven M. De Ciantis and Michael J. Kirton. A psychometric reexamination of Kolb's experiential learning cycle construct: A separation of level, style, and process. *Educational and Psychological Measurement*, 56:5, 1996, pp. 809-820.

The authors argue that Kolb's (1984) experiential learning theory inadvertently confuses three theoretically unrelated cognitive elements—style, level (abilities or capacity), and process. Kolb began by identifying a learning cycle process, whereby learners acquire information by immediate *concrete experience*, organize and examine the data through *reflective observation*, develop generalizations through *abstract conceptualization*, and then use those generalizations as guides during *active experimentation*. He then derived two bipolar dimensions by opposite pairing of four stages: prehension (concrete experience-abstract conceptualization) and transformation (reflective observation-active experimentation).

The quadrants formed by crossing these two dimensions are put forth as four learning styles. The authors suggest that the four-stage learning cycle and the four quadrants formed by the bipolar dimensions offer different views of individual differences in learning styles. The former would focus on an individual's ability to perform at each of the four stages (that is, the ideal learner would possess maximum abilities at all stages). The latter would focus on the manner or style in which each stage of the learning process is approached.

The authors argue further that a measure of learning styles can only support one of these views. They propose that the outcomes of a psychometric analysis of measures of the four stages would lead to different interpretations: (1) Measures of the four stages are uncorrelated, indicating four discrete constructs and leading to a four-stage process interpretation. (2) Each measure is negatively correlated with one other and uncorrelated with the remaining two, indicating a bi-bipolar orthogonal style interpretation. (3) All four measures are moderately correlated with one another, indicating that they are facets of the same underlying ability (a level interpretation).

These three interpretations were tested with data from 185 managers who took the *Learning Styles Questionnaire (LSQ)*. After refining the four scales of this instrument, the resulting data supported a learning-style interpretation (although the bipolar dimensions were not exactly the same as in Kolb's conceptualization). The authors concluded that the two independent style dimensions on the *LSQ* represent the way each stage of the learning cycle is approached rather than representing a preference for a particular stage.

Richard D. Freedman and Stephen A. Stumpf. Learning style theory: Less than meets the eye. *Academy of Management Review*, 5:3, 1980, pp. 445-447.

The authors note that Kolb's (refer to later book by Kolb, 1984) learning style theory and its associated *Learning Style Inventory (LSI)* has attracted the attention of researchers and educators interested in experiential learning. Despite its face validity, the authors raise questions about the empirical evidence in support of the theory. They question the lack of published results, the importance of findings based on small effect sizes, low test-retest reliability of the *LSI*, weak support for the two bipolar dimensions that are prominent in the theory, and a scoring system that can lead to erroneous support of the theory. The authors conclude that judgments about educational practices based on the theory should be suspended until the issues they raise are addressed.

A response to the Freedman and Stumpf article was published by the same journal in the following year:

David A. Kolb. Experiential learning theory and the *Learning Style Inventory*: A reply to Freedman and Stumpf. *Academy of Management Review*, 6:2, 1981, pp. 289-296.

Kolb addresses what he considers inaccuracies in the Freedman and Stumpf article, responds to their claim that there is little empirical support of experiential learning theory, and clarifies the relationship between the nature of the theory and the structure of the *Learning Style Inventory (LSI)*. Kolb criticizes Freedman and Stumpf for concluding that experiential learning theory is invalid because they believe the *LSI* is unreliable and improperly constructed. He cites the numerous research articles and dissertations on experiential learning that make use of the *LSI*. He also points out that there has been substantial empirical support for the theory of experiential learning generated by others who have used different methods and operationalization of constructs. Furthermore, Kolb maintains that the psychological testing criteria of independence of constructs and stability over time are inappropriate in assessing the utility of the *LSI*, which is derived from a theory based on assumptions of interdependence and variability.

John Hayes and Christopher W. Allinson. Cultural differences in the learning styles of managers. *Management International Review*, 28:3, 1988, pp. 75-80.

This articles focuses on the effects of culture on managers' learning styles. The authors argue that, of the many external agents that affect the learning styles of managers, one's cultural background may be an important influence. In order to test this hypothesis, the learning styles of 223 managers from twenty countries were assessed using the *Learning Styles Questionnaire (LSQ)*. This instrument was designed by Honey and Mumford (1989) to distinguish between four learning styles: Theorist, Pragmatist, Activist, and Reflector. For the purposes of this study, these four learning styles were collapsed into two dimensions: (1) the analysis dimension, which measures the extent to which a learner uses theory-building and testing methods (the Theorist style), versus a more intuitive approach (the Pragmatist style); and (2) the action dimension, which measures one's preference for trial-and-error approaches (the Activist style), versus a more contemplative approach (the Reflector style).

Three broad cultural categories—East Africa, India, and the United Kingdom (U.K.)—were represented in the sample of managers participating in the study. The action scores were highest for managers from the U.K. and lowest for East African managers. The analysis scores were highest for Indian managers while there were no differences between managers from East Africa and the U.K. on this dimension. The authors conclude that, indeed, culture plays an important role in managers' learning styles and it should be considered within the aim and content of managerial development activities.

David A. Kolb. *Experiential learning: Experience as the source of learning and development.* Englewood Cliffs, NJ: Prentice Hall, 1984, 256 pages.

In this book, Kolb describes experiential learning and proposes a model of the underlying structure of the learning process. This structural model leads to a typology of individual learning styles. The book is divided into three main sections: the historical roots of the model, the structure of the learning process and the resulting learning styles, and the relationship between learning and adult development.

In describing the historical roots of his experiential learning model, Kolb focuses on the work of John Dewey, Kurt Lewin, and Jean Piaget. He points out similarities among these three in their perspectives on learning. (1) Learning is best conceived as a process, not in terms of outcomes. (2) Learning is a continuous process grounded in experience. (3) The process of learning requires the resolution of conflicts between dialectically opposed modes of adaptation to the world. (4) Learning is a holistic process of adaptation to the world. (5) Learning involves transactions between the person and the environment. (6) Learning is the process of creating knowledge.

Kolb's model of experiential learning is based on a learning-process model referred to as the learning cycle. In this four-stage cycle, the learner moves from concrete experience to reflective observation to abstract conceptualization and then to active experimentation. He describes two structural dimensions underlying this learning cycle: the prehension dimension (how experience is grasped), anchored on one end by concrete experience and on the other by abstract conceptualization; and the transformation dimension (how experience is transformed into knowledge), anchored on one end by active experimentation and on the other by reflective observation. Kolb provides evidence from philosophy, psychology, and physiology to support the primacy of these two dimensions. The two dimensions are combined to yield four learning styles:

1. *Convergers* (abstract conceptualization combined with active experimentation) are specialists in problem solving, decision making, and the practical applications of ideas. They are best at problems with a single answer such as those found in traditional intelligence tests.

2. *Divergers* (concrete experience combined with reflective observation) rely on imagination and awareness of meaning to guide their problem solving. They value observation over action and are best at the generation of ideas, as in brainstorming, and at uncovering their implications.

3. *Assimilators* (abstract conceptualization combined with reflective observation) excel in the creation of theoretical models. They focus on ideas and abstract concepts and care less about the practicality of their ideas than about their soundness and precision.

4. *Accommodators* (concrete experience combined with active experimentation) enjoy doing things and carrying out plans and tasks. Their problem-solving approach tends to rely on trial-and-error.

Kolb posits that, over time, people develop stable strategies for grasping and transforming experience and thus develop preferences for one of these four learning styles. He presents research findings that show how the four learning styles are related to personality, early educational specialization, professional career choices, current job, and adaptive competencies.

According to Kolb, dominance of one learning style results in less-than-optimal learning, and thus development requires integration of the two polarities—concrete experience with abstract conceptualization, and active experimentation with reflective observation. He proposes a three-stage development process: acquisition, specialization, and integration. Kolb concludes with chapters focusing on the implications of his theory for higher education and for the challenge of lifelong learning.

Alan Mumford. Four approaches to learning from experience. *Industrial and Commercial Training*, 27:8, 1995, pp. 12-19.

This article describes a research project that analyzed how executives approach learning from experience. It is based on a series of one-on-one discussions conducted with twenty-one executives over a three-month period. The discussions were structured around their recent work activities, what they had learned from these activities, and how they had learned it.

Mumford and his colleagues identified four approaches to managerial learning among these executives: (1) The *intuitive approach* or learning from experience that is not conscious. Executives using this approach see learning as an inevitable outcome of having experiences. They find it difficult and unnecessary to articulate what they have learned or how they learned it and see no value in making the process more explicit. (2) The *incidental approach* involves learning by chance from experiences that are surprising or unexpected. The executive is jolted into examining the experience, usually in an informal way, and often prefers debriefing the experience with others. (3) The *retrospective approach* involves looking back over an experience and reaching conclusions about it. Although this approach, like the incidental approach, is often stimulated by an unexpected outcome, executives using it are also inclined to examine routine events and successes. (4) The *prospective approach* is defined as planning to learn before an experience takes place. Executives who use this approach viewed future events as opportunities to learn and were constantly tuned in to the possibility of learning. Although any executive might use multiple approaches, Mumford found that a number of them had a preference for one of the four approaches.

Mumford also noted that the kind of learning that executives gained from their experiences fell into three broad categories: knowledge, skills, and insights. More insight learning was reported with the "hindsight" approaches (intuitive, incidental, and retrospective), whereas learning from the prospective approach was more balanced between knowledge and insight learning.

Mumford concluded that the notion of learning styles is useful but covers only part of the learning domain. More focus on *how* individuals learn will yield knowledge useful for increasing the productivity of learning from experience. The practice of providing managers with developmental assignments should be supplemented by helping managers develop the learning processes necessary for the experience to be fully utilized.

Jose Eulogio Romero, Bennett J. Tepper, and Linda A. Tetrault. Development and validation of new scales to measure Kolb's (1985) learning style dimensions. *Educational and Psychological Measurement*, 52:2, 1992, pp. 171-180.

Given the psychometric shortcomings of existing measures of Kolb's (1985) learning styles, the authors propose a new measure. The measure was designed to overcome two critical issues in the existing operationalization of learning styles: measurement format and scale dimensionality. Ipsative (where people are forced to either end or to both ends of the scale) ranking formats, as with Kolb's *Learning Style Inventory* (1984), can produce artifactual relationships with dependent variables. The authors also argue that it is inappropriate to operationalize four modes of learning (as the *Learning Style Inventory* does) when the experiential learning theory posits two dimensions relevant to learning. Thus the authors constructed a normative, two-dimensional instrument to measure learning style.

Items for the questionnaire were based on Kolb's description of learners who emphasized each of the four learning styles. Complementary pairs of anchor statements (for instance, "I am a doer" versus "I am a watcher") were identified; seven corresponded to Kolb's reflection versus action dimension and seven corresponded to the concreteness versus abstractness dimension. Internal consistency, test-retest stability, factor structure, and predictive validity of the new measure were examined in two samples. The predictive validity analysis involved examining the relationships between learning styles and college majors.

The current research provided support for the reliability, dimensionality, and validity of the new measure. The authors caution, however, that the research should be considered as a first step in developing a psychometrically sound measure of learning styles.

Section 2.2: Ability to Learn from Experience

Kerry A. Bunker and Amy D. Webb. *Learning how to learn from experience: Impact of stress and coping.* Greensboro, NC: Center for Creative Leadership, 1992, 92 pages.

This report explores the relationship between coping with stress and learning from experience. It draws on two research studies: one that focused on managerial stress and coping in a corporate setting, and an exploratory study of how managers learn. The authors hypothesized that most learning events and developmental experiences are stressful. They suggest that the learning process requires overcoming the inertia associated with previously successful behavior (referred to as "going against the grain") and that maximum learning is obtained when individuals are strong and secure enough to make themselves vulnerable to the stresses and setbacks in the learning process. The bulk of the report focuses on factors that differentiate those managers who are better able to overcome inertia and cope with stress from those who are less able to do so.

The Managerial Stress Research Project collected stress and coping data from 246 managers in a major utility organization. Multiple methods, perspectives, and measures were used to answer the question, "How do managers adjust to and cope with the demands of living their total lives?" Four groups of managers were identified based on their overall levels of stress and how well they coped with the stress: Whiners (low stress, low adjustment),

Avoiders (high stress, low adjustment), Attackers (high stress, high adjustment), and Adaptors (low stress, high adjustment). Managers in these four groups differed in terms of personality, how they experienced stressors, the defense mechanisms and coping strategies they used, and their overall psychological health.

This framework was applied to an exploratory study directed toward understanding the processes managers use as they try to learn from their experiences. Avoiders did not welcome learning experiences; they felt overwhelmed by them. Their low self-esteem led them to expect failure. Their coping strategies emphasized reducing symptoms and finding ways to feel better. Thus, their learning was minimal. Attackers welcome stress, seek it out, and see the positives in stressful situations. They meet learning opportunities head-on with action strategies and optimism, and are skillful at drawing lessons from both successful and unsuccessful initiatives. Their action-oriented strategies can sometimes get them into trouble when the learning situation calls for them to first develop strategies or get input from others. The Adaptors are flexible learners, selecting their responses to fit the problems encountered. They also approach learning opportunities with optimism and can jump right in with action-oriented strategies, but unlike the Attacker, they are also comfortable delaying action while strategies are reviewed or involvement from others is sought. Adaptors are calm, controlled, and unworried. In learning situations, they ask questions to clarify their thinking, sort through new information, and are both open to and seek feedback.

The authors conclude with coping strategies for encouraging positive reactions to the stress of a learning challenge. For example, they suggest tackling stressors head-on rather than avoiding them, being flexible in shifting strategies to suit the problems encountered, and looking at life as a series of ongoing learning experiences.

Marilyn W. Daudelin. Learning from experience through reflection. *Organizational Dynamics*, 24:3, 1996, pp. 36-48.

The author builds a case for the benefits of reflection in organizations. According to Daudelin, the process of reflection "allows one to momentarily suspend the intense flow of new information to the brain. This enhances the processing of existing information, thereby better preparing the person to handle the demands of the rapidly changing environment" (p. 39). She proposes that reflection, as a way to learn, is a very natural process originating in ancient Greek philosophy that still plays an active part in modern organizations. Programs for total quality management, for example, constitute ways by which organizational members are allowed to stop and reflect on past actions and their consequences.

The reflection process can be separated into four stages: (1) articulation of the problem, (2) analysis of the problem, (3) formulation and testing of a theory to explain the problem, and (4) taking action to address the problem. The author argues that individuals vary in how they engage in that process: some tend to reflect alone, while others prefer to do so in small groups. For the sixty managers in the study, the process by which reflection was achieved influenced how much learning occurred. Managers could reflect by themselves, with a small group of peers, or with the help of a mentor. Reflecting alone or with a mentor were the most successful methods. Those who reflected with peers did not learn more than the control group (a group not instructed to reflect) and, in addition, reported less learning than the managers who used the first two methods.

The type of developmental experience (such as building something from nothing and leading a project assignment) or the length of that experience did not have any effect on the amount of learning reported. The authors hypothesized that the specific dynamics attached to peer-group interactions may have interfered with the process of reflection and limited the learning process.

This study highlights the benefits of reflection as a tool for learning from experience. It also underscores the importance of methodological issues for the success of reflection.

Kathleen Dechant. Knowing how to learn: The "neglected" management ability. *Journal of Management Development*, 9:4, 1990, pp. 40-49.

Dechant argues that to develop effective managers, we not only have to know what behaviors, abilities, and attitudes are needed by managers, but also how these things are learned. In this article, she focuses on the question, "What learning strategies and tactics do effective managers use as they go about managing?"

Twenty-one senior-level managers who had recently completed or who were more than halfway through challenging job assignments were interviewed about what they had learned from them. This group of managers had been identified by others in the organization as excellent managers who had been successful at managing change.

The primary learning strategy reported was self-directed learning, which took two forms: (1) techniques to identify learning goals, pursue learning experiences, and evaluate progress; and (2) changes in the assumptions, values, and feelings about themselves and about themselves in relation to others. With respect to the first form of self-directed learning, three specific competencies were important: (1) the ability to diagnose one's personal learning needs and those of others, (2) the ability to identify appropriate strategies and resources to meet one's own learning needs and those of others, and (3) the ability to collect and validate evidence of the accomplishment of learning. The changes in assumptions, values, and feelings clustered around four areas: influencing others, visioning, enhancing political acumen, and relationship forging.

The author concludes with a checklist that incorporates what the effective, self-directed learners in this study did. It can serve as a model for managers who want to be more effective learners and should be used particularly at the beginning of a new assignment.

John P. Kotter. *The new rules: How to succeed in today's post-corporate world*. New York: Free Press, 1995, 239 pages.

This book is based on the experiences of 115 Harvard MBAs from the class of 1974. The author followed the career choices, successes, and failures of these graduates for twenty years through the use of questionnaires and interviews. Kotter draws four main conclusions from this follow-up study: (1) What is required to succeed has been shifting over the past decade. (2) This shift is driven by many factors, the most important being globalization. (3) Those who are successful are engaged in career paths that are less linear, more dynamic, and more unstable that those who are not. (4) Success in these career paths requires high standards, self-confidence, and a willingness to learn.

This latter point is expanded upon in chapter 9, "Lifelong Learning." In this chapter, Kotter focuses on the willingness and ability to learn and grow beyond the completion of the MBA. Members of the class were told to expect a fairly linear career path. A typical path would involve an entry-level marketing assignment, followed by larger and larger marketing assignments, to finally shift into increasingly bigger general management positions. However, a majority of the class of '74 followed more chaotic trajectories involving a variety of assignments. These turbulent career paths were created by economic factors such as mergers, downsizing, new technologies, and foreign competition. However, the author notes that these paths were not only the results of volatile times, they were also explicitly sought as a source of learning. Most successful managers embraced these opportunities and did not shy away from them.

According to Kotter, one of the biggest obstacles to growth for the class of '74 is the lack of time. Investment in personal growth often competes with other demands and, for that reason, successful managers have devised strategies to cope with these demands. These strategies ranged from "buying" time (for example, hiring personal help) to delaying marriage and children until their late twenties and early thirties.

Victoria J. Marsick and Karen E. Watkins. *Informal and incidental learning in the workplace*. London: Rutledge, 1990, 270 pages.

Informal and incidental learning both refer to learning that takes place outside of formally structured classroom-based activities. These types of learning usually take place under nonroutine conditions, that is, when an individual's learned responses or habitual ways of acting are least likely to work. A distinction is made between these two types of learning. Incidental learning occurs as a byproduct of some other activity, such as task accomplishment or interpersonal interaction. It is never planned or intentional. Informal learning is more intentional, as in self-directed learning or when the help of a mentor or coach is sought.

The authors develop a theory of informal and incidental learning, and then illustrate and expand the theory through the description and analysis of six projects in which learning from experience was key. The building of the theory begins with the defining characteristics of informal and incidental learning: it is experience-based, nonroutine, and often tacit. The individual factors that are assumed to enhance informal and incidental learning are proactivity (a readiness to take initiative), critical reflectivity (the bringing of one's mental models to consciousness and critiquing them), and creativity (thinking beyond one's normal point of view). Building on the experiential learning cycle derived from various learning researchers' work, the authors propose a human resources learning cone to illustrate how informal and incidental learning permeates all other human resources activities within an organization.

Informal learning is examined more closely through three projects: (1) how Swedish managers learned from experience as they worked in teams on projects, (2) the learning of educational field workers promoting health and family planning, and (3) how a small group of adult educators learned aspects of their work. The incidental learning by human resources professionals in the course of their work is examined in three additional cases.

The authors conclude by providing a rationale for why human resources professionals should pay more attention to informal and incidental learning in the workplace and suggesting strategies for enhancing informal and incidental learning at the individual, group, organizational, and professional levels.

Morgan W. McCall, Jr. Identifying leadership potential in future international executives: Developing a concept. *Consulting Psychology Journal*, 46:1, 1994, pp. 49-63.

McCall argues that the qualities exhibited by the mature executive are not necessarily the same qualities a company should be looking for in a high-potential manager. If we accept that the skills of an international executive are developed over time, then potential might be better defined as the ability to take advantage of learning opportunities. Thus, this article develops a conceptual framework for assessing international executive potential by examining ability to learn from experience.

The author first reviews literature to support four key statements: (1) managers learn, grow, and change over the course of their careers; (2) some people learn, grow, and change more than others; (3) ability to learn is important to success; and (4) underlying processes of learning and growth do not vary by country.

To develop the "ability to learn" framework, forty-six experts in the identification of international executive potential were interviewed about what they look for when trying to identify people with potential. The interview data were analyzed from two perspectives. First, they were analyzed for themes, resulting in the identification of eleven dimensions executives look for when assessing executive potential in up-and-coming managers: sense of adventure, courageous, action oriented, analytically agile, special talent with people, broadly respected, know the business, passionate, resourceful, learn from mistakes, and open to learning. Because these dimensions were similar to those generated in studies of successful senior executives, it suggested that the experts did not tend to have a developmental perspective, but rather looked for the characteristics of successful executives in younger managers.

A second analysis of the interview data focused on characteristics that might identify people with the talent and motivation to learn from the developmental experiences they were given. From this analysis, people who are best able to learn from experience are described as having curiosity about how things work, a sense of adventure, hardiness, a bias toward action, acceptance of responsibility for learning and change, a respect for differences, an openness to feedback, and consistent growth over time. These eight dimensions were further grouped into three major factors that indicate a pattern of active learning: seeking out more experiences that provide learning opportunities, acting in ways that produce more information and feedback, and incorporating information on the impact of their experiences into future behavior.

McCall concludes with a model for the early identification of international executives that has three major components: individual attributes and skills, context (the content of assignments, how people are chosen for assignments, and the reward system for development), and time (for the accumulation of experience and learning).

Anne G. Perkins. The learning mind-set: Who's got it, what it's good for. *Harvard Business Review*, 72:2, 1994, pp. 11-12.

This article focuses on one group of managers identified in the Isabella and Forbes (1994) study of key events in executive careers, namely those identified as having a learning mind-set. Only 10% of the executives in their study were included in this subset. They were differentiated from other executives by numerous transformational events in their careers, agility of thought (ability to see solutions, adapt easily to new situations, and see patterns and connections between seemingly unconnected variables), a focus on learning, and communication style (nonlinear and ready use of metaphors and analogies). A subsequent study found executives with a learning mind-set to be particularly suited for managing strategic alliances. "There is something about the learning mind-set that allows the alliance manager to walk in and out of different cultures or situations with ease and to understand the intricate set of relationships needed for the alliance to succeed" (p. 12).

Marian N. Ruderman, Patricia J. Ohlott, and Cynthia D. McCauley. *Developing from job experiences: The role of self-esteem and self-efficacy*. Paper presented at the annual meeting of the Society for Industrial and Organizational Psychology, San Diego, 1996.

This paper focuses on the effects of self-esteem and self-efficacy on learning from challenging job experiences. The authors argue that because there is ample evidence that self-concept functions as an important determinant of motivation and action, it is an important area for exploring how individual-difference factors affect on-the-job development.

A sample of 261 managers indicated the degree to which they were experiencing various job challenges and what they were learning from their jobs. They also completed measures of self-esteem in the workplace (the value and worthiness individuals place on themselves as organizational members) and self-efficacy in their current jobs (the belief that one has the skills and abilities to perform well in one's current job).

Results indicated that self-esteem was positively related to reported development from job experiences, and self-efficacy was negatively related to development. In addition, both self-concept variables moderated the relationship between degree of job challenge and amount of on-the-job learning. The relationship between these two variables was stronger for managers with lower self-esteem, a finding that is consistent with behavioral plasticity theory (that is, individuals with lower self-esteem react with greater intensity to their work environments). The moderating role of self-efficacy was less clear, but the results suggested that managers with higher self-efficacy were more adversely affected by negative job challenges (for instance, inherited problems or lack of support).

The authors conclude with suggestions for enhancing managerial learning: develop a climate that values and encourages individual learning, help managers see that they have room for continued development, and realize that challenging assignments are particularly important for managers with moderate to low self-esteem.

Gretchen M. Spreitzer, Morgan W. McCall, and Joan D. Mahoney. Early identification of international executive potential. *Journal of Applied Psychology*, 82:1, 1997, pp. 6-29.

The authors argue that if international leadership skills are learned, any improvement in identifying people who learn from their experiences will aid in the selection of international executives. They propose that there are two sets of skills that may be used to predict the success of executives: "end-state competencies" and the ability to learn from experience. End-state competencies are specific skills and knowledge necessary for effective executive behavior; for example, "knowing the business" is an example of an end-state competency. The identification and usage of such competencies in selecting fast-trackers is sometimes counterproductive because the required skills and knowledge are subject to change over time; end-state competencies are often valued one day only to become obsolete the next. The ability to learn from experience, on the other hand, is not sensitive to fluctuations in organizational needs because effective learners, by definition, will be able to acquire new skills and knowledge with relative ease. In this context, it may be more useful than end-state competencies for early identification of executive potential. As stated by the authors, "The ability to learn from experience may prove to be more important than a high rating in a currently valued competency" (p. 6). This paper describes the development of a rating instrument for the early identification of international executives based on a learning-from-experience perspective.

Drawing heavily on previous work by McCall (1994), in addition to interviewing forty-six executives involved with the identification of international executive potential, the authors began by creating a set of items that captured the content domain of both end-states characteristics of executive potential and the ability to learn from experience. After pretesting the items, a final version of the survey instrument consisted of 116 items. This survey, called *Prospector*, was administered to the bosses of over 1,000 managers from six international companies located in twenty-one different countries. Both high-potential and solid-performing (but not likely to advance) managers at various organizational levels were included in the sample.

Factor analysis and interpretation resulted in fourteen factors being retained as scales. These scales represent fourteen dimensions for assessing executive potential: seeks opportunities to learn, acts with integrity, is sensitive to cultural differences, is committed to success, seeks broad business knowledge, brings out the best in people, is insightful (sees things from new angles), has the courage to take a stand, uses feedback, seeks feedback, takes risks, is culturally adventurous, is flexible, and is open to criticism.

The second phase of instrument development involved assessing the validity of the early identification measure. Several strategies were used for building validity evidence: testing the power of ratings on the fourteen scales to discriminate between high-potential and solid-performing managers, examining cultural differences in scores on the fourteen scales, and testing whether high-potential managers with expatriate experience are rated higher on the scales than are those without expatriate experience. Results from all three of these strategies provided initial validity evidence for the measure.

The authors point out areas for further research as their measure is refined: establishing evidence of predictive validity; extending samples beyond U.S., European, and Australian managers; understanding how contextual factors influence ability to learn from experience; and developing predictive models of career progression. The practical uses of the measure include developmental feedback for managers, content development for training and coaching programs, selection of high-potential managers, and structuring of significant job experiences to increase their learning potential.

Section 2.3: Demographic Differences

Mary Cianni and Beverly Romberger. Perceived racial, ethnic, and gender differences in access to developmental experiences. *Group and Organization Management*, 20:4, 1995, pp. 440-459.

This study focused on the differential effects of gender, race, and ethnicity on perceptions of access to developmental experiences provided by immediate supervisors. A total of 3,106 mid-level employees of a financial services organization were asked the extent to which their supervisor provided them with informal and formal developmental experiences, and how satisfied they were with their developmental opportunities. In the informal development category, the authors included the extent to which supervisors (1) provided assignments that increased contact with higher-level managers, (2) provided assignments designed to gain new skills, (3) promoted one's career in general and within one's unit, (4) provided information about the department or the company, (5) displayed similar values and attitudes, (6) encouraged the taking on of new responsibilities, and (7) served as a role model. In the formal developmental experiences category, the supervisor's support for participating in formal training and development programs, special projects, key meetings, and task forces were included.

The only gender difference found in the perception of access to informal development opportunities was on receiving department and company information; women reported that they perceived receiving less information than men reported. Men also reported more opportunities to attend external management development programs than did women. In addition, women were less satisfied than men with the developmental opportunities provided by their supervisors. Results from follow-up interviews revealed that female managers, more than male managers, felt that they must take charge of their own development.

A unique aspect of this study is the distinction made within the "minority" category resulting in separate analyses for African Americans, Hispanics, and Asians. This approach proved useful because most findings did not generalize across ethnicity. African-American employees perceived less encouragement from their supervisors to assume new responsibility than their white counterparts. They also reported less similarity to their supervisors in terms of values and attitudes. On the other hand, African Americans reported more participation in external development programs than whites. Hispanics reported fewer assignments to special projects and fewer assignments involving increased contact with higher-level managers than whites. No significant effects were found for Asian employees. The authors also reported that tenure was negatively related to many developmental factors such as the provision of new assignments and supervisor's encouragement of new opportunity.

One implication noted is the importance of separating the various racial, ethnic, and gender groups for investigation. The perceptions, beliefs, and needs of managers seem to vary according to gender, race, and ethnicity. Moreover, supervisors need to pay greater attention to any unintentional biases in the assignment of both formal and informal development opportunities.

Dianne D. Horgan. A cognitive learning perspective on women becoming expert managers. *Journal of Business and Psychology*, 3:3, 1989, pp. 299-313.

The author uses a cognitive learning framework to analyze the task facing women managers. She argues that the inherent complexity embedded in the role of women managers can help explain why women have difficulty in achieving top executive positions.

The paper begins with an explanation of how individuals develop expertise through extensive experience. First, novices learn facts and rules that are applied across situations without considering the need for exceptions. As they gain experience, they learn exceptions to their rules and begin to internalize rules. Progressing further requires a great deal of high-quality experience and feedback. As expertise is developed, information is organized in more sophisticated ways, and the individual sees new situations in terms of familiar abstract and complex patterns. The author argues that, in the realm of management, the movement from novice to expert is harder for women.

One reason for this increased difficulty is that managerial expertise requires much social learning, and the social system differs for men and women. As a woman manager observes other managers in a wide variety of situations, she must analyze each behavior, not just in terms of its effectiveness but also for its gender appropriateness (if a woman engages in the same behavior, will it be just as effective?). Learning from their own experiences can also be more difficult for women. In analyzing what works and doesn't work in a situation, women managers must separate the task-relevant information from the task-irrelevant information. (For instance, did an action fail because it was a bad idea or because it was not well received because she is female?)

Contributing to these difficulties is the small number of high-level female executives who are available to serve as role models. As a result, women have fewer opportunities to observe same-sex behavior across a variety of situations, thus decreasing their ability to develop useful heuristics or recognize complex patterns. Women are also less likely to get the high-quality, task-relevant feedback necessary for becoming an expert manager. It is often difficult for male managers to diagnose the reasons for a woman's poor performance because they, too, have only frameworks for understanding how a male could have been successful in the situation.

The author concludes that "women necessarily will have more difficulty obtaining feedback, will receive less helpful feedback, will often be presented with ambiguous patterns of behavior, and will always have a smaller sample of role model behavior" (p. 312). She suggests that the obvious solution is to increase the number of women in management. Acknowledging that this will not happen overnight, she suggests that in the meantime we recognize that in the business world women's tasks are more difficult to learn than men's. To support their learning, women need longer evaluation periods, more access to female mentors and role models, and male bosses who are more sensitive to the different social circumstances surrounding men and women and who can better separate task-relevant and task-irrelevant behaviors.

Karen S. Lyness and Donna E. Thompson. Above the glass ceiling: A comparison of matched samples of female and male executives. *Journal of Applied Psychology,* 82:3, 1997, pp. 359-375.

Much has been written about the glass-ceiling effect on the careers of female managers. Of the many factors that contribute to the glass ceiling, the lack of developmental opportunities provided to female managers is one of the most important. Women middle-managers have been found to experience fewer developmental challenges than men of comparable rank, leading to a reduced representation in executive positions. This article focuses on those female managers that have actually made it into the executive suite and that have successfully broken through the glass ceiling. A sample of fifty-one females from this select group (less than 5% of high-level executives) is compared to a comparable sample of fifty-six male executives on a variety of dimensions such as authority level, compensation, career history, and job attitudes. Each executive also completed a shortened version of the *Developmental Challenge Profile (DCP)*, an instrument used to measure developmental characteristics of jobs (see McCauley, Ruderman, Ohlott, & Morrow, 1994). Executives in the two samples were drawn from the same organization and matched for age, position, performance level, and pay.

The findings of this study "suggest that there are more similarities than differences between these female executives and their male counterparts" (p. 25). For example, no differences were found in bonus pay and most work attitudes. These results differ somewhat from previous research that uncovered substantial differences between male and female executives. The authors explain these results on their matching procedure, which ensured that the two groups were identical on key organizational characteristics.

Despite the lack of differences for most measures, meaningful differences did surface in areas related to developmental experiences. Female executives held jobs with less authority than their male counterparts; female executives had a significantly lower number of subordinates than males. During their careers, female executives were also less likely to have moved within the organization and to have obtained an overseas assignment. Related to that, female executives were less positive toward their future career opportunities within the organization. Finally, male executives scored higher on "Handling External Pressure," a *DCP* dimension known to contribute to development in higher-level positions.

It appears that, despite the substantial achievement of breaking the glass ceiling and making it into the executive suite, female managers still face some basic inequalities. These results provide evidence to support the presence of a higher, second glass ceiling that further impedes the development of female executives.

Patricia J. Ohlott, Marian N. Ruderman, and Cynthia D. McCauley. Gender differences in managers' developmental job experiences. *Academy of Management Journal*, 37:1, 1994, pp. 46-67.

Differences in on-the-job development opportunities have been suggested as a reason why so few women have been promoted to senior management positions in corporations. The goal of this study was to enhance understanding of these possible gender differences by using quantitative methods to look at specific developmental job experiences.

The *Developmental Challenge Profile (DCP)*, an instrument that measures a manager's perceptions of the developmental components in his or her current job, was completed by 281 men and 226 women. The authors statistically controlled for age, job tenure, familiarity with the job, education level, and job type in order to isolate gender as the variable of interest.

The scales on the *DCP* are grouped into five categories: job transitions, creating change, high levels of responsibility, nonauthority relationships, and obstacles. No gender differences were found on the job transition scales. In addition, there were no differences on scales related to creating change (developing new directions, inherited problems, reduction decisions, and problems with employees). The authors interpreted these results as evidence of progress in that women managers seem to be gaining access to these types of challenging assignments.

However, differences were found on several scales reflecting high levels of responsibility (high stakes, managing business diversity, and handling external pressure); men rated their jobs as having more of these components than women did. The authors suggest that this finding may point to a more subtle form of gender bias in access to developmental assignments; women may be reaching the same levels in organizations but may not be getting key assignments that involve making critical decisions, visibility, breadth of responsibilities, and external interactions.

Women also reported more lack of personal support in their jobs than did men. Thus, women continue to feel left out of important networks, have difficulty finding supportive people to talk to, and feel they must continually fight to be recognized for the work they do. The authors argue that these factors may be a result of moving talented women quickly up the management ranks with the unintended consequences of higher turnover and failure rates among them.

Patricia J. Ohlott and Lorrina J. Eastman. *Age differences in developmental job experiences: Evidence of a gray ceiling?* Paper presented at the annual meeting of the Academy of Management, Dallas, TX, 1994.

Older workers may face a "gray ceiling" that denies them equal employment opportunities. For example, there is some evidence that older employees are discriminated against in terms of access to formal training. In this paper, the authors extended this inquiry of age bias by examining the relationship between age and access to challenging job experiences.

Using a sample of 973 managers, the extent to which age was related to each of the sixteen scales on the *Developmental Challenge Profile (DCP)* was investigated. The authors controlled for organizational level, gender, and job tenure. Results showed that age was negatively related to eight of the scales and positively related to three.

In discussing these results, the sixteen scales on the *DCP* were clustered into four broad categories of job challenges: job transitions, task-related challenges, obstacles, and support. Older managers rated their jobs lower than did younger managers on both scales related to job transitions: unfamiliar responsibilities and proving yourself. This is an important finding because job transitions provide some of the most potent developmental opportunities.

On the task-related dimension of the *DCP*, age was negatively related to five scales (problem employees, inherited problems, job overload, high stakes, and influencing without authority) and positively related to two scales (reduction decision and handling external pressure). The authors offer three possible explanations for the negative relationships: (1) older managers may have mastered these tasks, therefore they are no longer challenged by them; (2) older managers take on fewer of these tasks than do younger managers; and (3) older managers are not selected for these types of developmental assignments. Moreover, the authors argue that reduction decisions and handling external pressure, on which older managers scored higher, may reflect changes that the entire organization is experiencing and for which older managers are less prepared.

Finally, older managers scored lower than younger managers on one obstacle scale (difficult boss) and higher on the supportive boss scale. Again, a variety of explanations are posited for this finding, including higher relationship-management skills, better person-organization fit, and less need for support among older managers.

The authors concluded that the needs of older managers in terms of developmental assignments are not totally being met. They suggest that organizations should provide older managers with more job transitions and more start-up and turnaround assignments.

Ellen Van Velsor and Martha W. Hughes. *Gender differences in the development of managers: How women managers learn from experience.* Greensboro, NC: Center for Creative Leadership, 1990, 43 pages.

The authors compared two studies of executive development—one that focused almost exclusively on men (McCall et al., 1988) and one that replicated the men's study with women (Morrison et al., 1987)—in order to better understand gender differences associated with experiential learning. They examined whether there were differences in the way men and women learned through their job experiences; and whether there were differences between men and women in what is learned from these experiences.

In each study, successful managers described key events in their careers and what they had learned from these events. The authors compared the responses from 78 women with those from 189 men. The framework for categorizing the events and lessons was first developed from the men's study and then applied to data from the women.

To compare the types of lessons men and women reported learning from their experiences, the authors focused on the twelve lesson categories most frequently reported by the two groups. Seven of the categories were the same for men and women (for example, directing and motivating employees, self-confidence, and basic management values). The remaining top lessons for women reflected efforts to discover who they were as individuals in their organizations, whereas those for men reflected mastering new skills that related directly to job performance. The authors argue that the more complex working environment faced by women (namely, less organizational experience, minority status, the need to define sex-role-appropriate behavior, isolation, and discrimination) forces them to struggle with and thus learn more about how they fit into the organization.

The key events at the source of these lessons were also contrasted across gender. Most of the developmental experiences reported by men can be grouped into three large categories: assignments, other people, and hardships. More of men's than women's learning was derived from assignments (43% and 60%), but more of women's than men's came from other people (28% and 14%) and hardships (22% and 16%).

Looking within the three main categories of experience, the authors found both quantitative and qualitative differences between men and women. In terms of assignments, women reported experiencing far fewer turnaround or start-from-scratch assignments. Line-to-staff switches seemed to be less potent for women, whereas managing a larger-scope job and project/task force assignments appeared to be richer learning experiences for them. In terms of learning from others, over 50% of the women reported at least one key event involving learning from a boss; only 18% of men reported such an event. Although women may report learning more from others because they had fewer assignment experiences to draw on, the authors point out that there is growing evidence that women may be more inclined than men to learn from others. Finally, business mistakes was the only hardship event that women reported at a different rate than men (22% for women, 11% for men). However, other hardship events contained some qualitative differences; for example, more women attributed their career setback experiences to their gender.

The authors noted that challenging assignments can help or hurt development, depending on the amount and context; thus, organizations need to find the balance between too much challenge and insufficient challenge. The data in this study, however, suggest that organizations have been too cautious toward women in the past. The authors conclude that the best mix for development is challenge combined with ample support. They caution that the influx of women into lower and middle levels of management may decrease special efforts to support the development of women, a move they believe would be a serious mistake.

Connections

Experiential Learning Cycle

Although the experiential learning cycle is most often associated with Kolb's (1984) work on learning and learning styles, its roots can be traced (as Kolb does) to Kurt Lewin's[3] model of action research, John Dewey's (1938) model of learning, and Jean Piaget's[4] model of cognitive development. What these models have in common is a view of learning as a continuous process grounded in experience and personal development as a process of adaptation to the world. A person is engaged in an ongoing process of having concrete experiences, making observations and reflecting on that experience, forming concepts and generalizations based on those reflections, and testing those ideas in new situations.

---

[3] Kurt Lewin. *Field theory in social sciences.* New York: Harper and Row, 1951.

[4] Jean Piaget. *Psychology and epistemology.* Middlesex, England: Penguin, 1971.

These views have influenced others who have developed similar notions of learning cycles. Kelly (1955) viewed learning as a theory-building process in which hypotheses about the world are formed, tested in practice, and then modified according to the results. Argyris and Schon's (1974) concept of single-loop and double-loop learning extended the cycle concept to distinguish between experiences that lead to the detection and correction of errors in theories from those that invoke the reexamination of basic principles that govern the purpose of those theories. Processes similar to the individual experiential learning cycle have been used to describe organizational learning (Argyris & Schon, 1978; Dixon, 1994; Kim, 1993), managerial work (Wilson, O'Hare, & Shipper, 1990), consulting processes (Schein, 1987), and methods of scientific inquiry (Argyris, Putnam, & Smith, 1987).

With the experiential learning cycle as a framework, it would come as no surprise that on-the-job experiences are a primary driver of managerial learning, growth, and change. This theoretical perspective is highly consistent with the notion that work and learning are tightly intertwined. But it also suggests that learning is an active process, highly dependent on the individual's initiative, interpretation of situations, powers of observation, ability to reflect on thinking processes, and willingness to test hypotheses.

Chris Argyris, Robert Putnam, and Diana McLain Smith. *Action science.* San Francisco: Jossey-Bass, 1987, 480 pages.

Chris Argyris and Donald A. Schön. *Theory in practice: Increasing professional effectiveness.* San Francisco: Jossey-Bass, 1974, 224 pages.

Chris Argyris and Donald A. Schön. *Organizational learning: A theory of action perspective.* Reading, MA: Addison-Wesley, 1978, 344 pages.

Nancy M. Dixon. *The organizational learning cycle: How we can learn collectively.* London: McGraw-Hill, 1994, 141 pages.

George A. Kelly. *The psychology of personal constructs.* New York: Norton, 1955, 1,218 pages.

Daniel H. Kim. The link between individual and organizational learning. *Sloan Management Review*, 35:1, 1993, pp. 37-50.

Edward H. Schein. *Process consultation, vol. II: Lessons for managers and consultants.* Reading, MA: Addison-Wesley, 1987, 208 pages.

Clark L. Wilson, Donal O'Hare, and Frank Shipper. Task cycle theory: The processes of influence. In K. E. Clark & M. B. Clark (Eds.), *Measures of leadership.* West Orange, NJ: Leadership Library of America, 1990, pp. 185-204.

Learning to Learn

Scholars and practitioners in the field of education have also had an obvious interest in the process of learning. Within the last twenty years, the concept of "learning to learn" has become more prominent in this field. The term is used somewhat differently by different writers, but in general refers to the processes by which individuals become more effective learners. Although most often conceived of as learning how to learn in educational settings, some authors have expanded the concept to include self-directed learning outside of educational settings and to learning how to learn from life experiences. There has also been growing acceptance that the major goal of the educational system is to expand learning-to-learn capacities in individuals that will serve them throughout their lives. These capacities are metacognitive in nature, that is, they enable individuals to reflect on, monitor, and evaluate their learning processes and their progress on learning tasks.

In reviewing the literature on learning to learn, Candy (1990) noted several themes related to the concept: (1) learning to learn is a lifelong process; (2) it is a developmental process in which people's understanding of learning evolves; (3) it involves acquiring attitudes, frameworks, and skills that allow individuals to become more flexible and self-directed learners in a variety of contexts; (4) it is developed as one is engaged in learning endeavors; (5) it may be enhanced through formal schooling; (6) in its most advanced forms, it leads to critical awareness of the assumptions and expectations that influence how people perceive knowledge; (7) it has both generic and context-specific facets; and (8) its meaning varies according to the meaning given to the word "learning."

One of the most comprehensive models of the learning-to-learn process is offered by Gibbons (1990). The model is three-dimensional; it looks at the kind of learning being engaged in, the learning domain, and the forms of learning. Of most relevance to our understanding of individual variability in on-the-job learning is a delineation of the elements of the three forms of learning: reason, emotion, and action. For example, the key elements of the role of reason in learning how to learn are observing, analyzing, weighing evidence, creating new ideas, and reflecting. Gibbons posits that those individuals who learn to do these things better will be more effective learners.

The learning-to-learn literature that does focus on learning beyond the classroom can inform our understanding of the learning strategies and metacognitive abilities that might enhance on-the-job learning. Because most of the writers are focused on education, the literature also suggests how the learning strategies can be taught and metacognitive abilities enhanced.

Stephen D. Brookfield. *Understanding and facilitating adult learning.* San Francisco: Jossey-Bass, 1986, 375 pages.

Philip C. Candy. How people learn to learn. In R. M. Smith (Ed.), *Learning to learn across the lifespan.* San Francisco: Jossey-Bass, 1990, pp. 30-63.

Edward Cell. *Learning to learn from experience.* Albany: State University of New York Press, 1984, 245 pages.

Sylvia Downs, Howard S. Barrows, and Robert M. Smith. *Learning management: Emerging directions for learning to learn in the workplace.* Columbus: National Center for Research on Vocational Education, The Ohio State University, 1987, 57 pages.

Maurice Gibbons. A working model of the learning-how-to-learn process. In R. M. Smith (Ed.), *Learning to learn across the lifespan.* San Francisco: Jossey-Bass, 1990, pp. 64-97.

Malcolm S. Knowles. *Self-directed learning.* New York: Association Press, 1975, 135 pages.

Robert M. Smith, Ed. *Learning to learn across the lifespan.* San Francisco: Jossey-Bass, 1990, 382 pages.

Allen Tough. *The adult's learning projects.* Toronto, Canada: Ontario Institute for Studies in Education, 1971, 191 pages.

SECTION 3: USING DEVELOPMENTAL ASSIGNMENTS

Overview

This section describes applications of developmental job experiences within organizations. We outline here the many ways that organizations attempt to intentionally and systematically use developmental assignments and help managers learn from these assignments.

Interest in developmental assignments has grown in recent years. This growth is probably the result of a combination of many factors. For one, organizations are putting increasing value on human capital and managerial development and are thus more open to the use of alternative techniques such as developmental assignments. Second, as managerial positions become more complex, traditional training programs often fall short of providing the adequate knowledge and the tools necessary for optimal managerial develop-ment. Third, upward mobility and its inherent challenges, such as increasing responsibilities and visibility, are decreasing as organizations become flatter and opportunities for advancement are declining; developmental assignments allow for the infusion of new responsibilities and challenges that would not otherwise be available for most managers.

The publications included in this section range from case studies to descriptions of techniques and tools that can assist in the implementation of management development through work experiences. Although a total of eighteen articles or books are included in this section, it seems safe to assume that most of the applications that use developmental assignments are not found in the popular literature. In some organizations, assignment-based developmental efforts may be conducted on a small scale—too small to warrant publishing. The protection of programs believed to represent a competitive advantage may prevent the dissemination of some useful infor-mation about the use of developmental assignments in organizations. Also, many of these efforts may never be institutionalized on a formal basis. In sum, the content of this chapter probably represents only a small portion of all the work that has been done in this area; however, the publications presented here should, at a minimum, capture the diversity of developmental efforts centered on job experience in organizations and at the same time provide a series of tools and techniques that have been used in support of these efforts.

In the "Connections" section, we also provide an extensive list of publications on action learning, a specific educational strategy that incorpo-rates work on specific organizational problems into management training programs. Action-learning programs represent an additional way in which organizations can use work experiences for management development.

Key Findings and Implications

There are multiple ways to systematically and intentionally use developmental assignments.

A variety of approaches exist when it comes to using developmental assignments. We found articles that described a particular company's intentional efforts to use assignments for management development (Clark & Lyness, 1991; Cobb & Gibbs, 1990; Friedman, 1990; Northcraft, Griffith, & Shalley, 1992; Seibert, Hall, & Kram, 1995) and ones that advocated more general strategies for systematically using developmental assignments (Bonoma & Lawler, 1989; Hall, 1995; Lombardo & Eichinger, 1990; McCauley, Eastman, & Ohlott, 1995; Morrison & Hock, 1986; Stewart, 1984; White, 1992). Across both types of articles, three general approaches emerged. (1) When choosing people for jobs—particularly when these choices are part of a succession planning system—use the potential development offered by the job as one factor in the decision-making process (Clark & Lyness, 1991; Friedman, 1990; McCauley et al., 1995). (2) Use targeted assignments as part of a management development system (Bonoma & Lawler, 1989; Clark & Lyness, 1991; Cobb & Gibbs, 1990; Morrison & Hock, 1986; Northcraft et al., 1992; Seibert et al., 1995; Stewart, 1984; White, 1992). (3) Develop people by adding challenge to their current jobs (Hall, 1995; Lombardo & Eichinger, 1990; White, 1992). The second approach ("use targeted assignments") includes strategies for targeting assignments to develop competencies that a company has deemed as strategically important, such as identifying assignments to use for developing global leaders or for developing strategic thinkers. And it includes systems for the long-term development of people in particular career paths or individuals targeted for higher management jobs.

According to the authors of these articles, the systematic and intentional use of developmental assignments calls for:

1. *The identification of key assignments that will serve the general or specific developmental needs of managers.* Some authors offer examples of assignments targeted for particular developmental needs (Bonoma & Lawler, 1989; Lombardo & Eichinger, 1990; Seibert et al., 1995; Stewart, 1984). For example, Seibert et al.

describe how 3M Company uses international experience, in the form of managing a subsidiary in a foreign country, to develop global perspectives in its high-potential managers. Others offer strategies organizations could use to identify developmental assignments in their own setting (Hall, 1995; McCauley et al., 1995; Morrison & Hock, 1986; Northcraft et al., 1992; White, 1992). For example, White suggests interviewing senior managers about their developmental experiences, and McCauley et al. (1995) suggest gathering data from former job incumbents.

2. *Matching individuals to jobs based on their developmental needs.* Developmental needs might be identified for a whole group of managers (Bonoma & Lawler, 1989; Clark & Lyness, 1991; Cobb & Gibbs, 1990; Friedman, 1990; Seibert et al., 1995). For example, the Oklahoma Department of Corrections identified decision making as an area in need of development for all its younger managers (Friedman, 1990). Developmental needs can also be diagnosed for individual managers; and new jobs, temporary assignments, or added challenges can be selected to remedy those unique needs (Lombardo & Eichinger, 1990; McCauley et al., 1995; White, 1992).

3. *Embedding the use of assignments in a larger management development system.* Such a management development system should first and foremost be aligned with the organization's business strategy (Clark & Lyness, 1991; Hall, 1995; Morrison & Hock, 1986; Seibert et al., 1995). It should also link assignments with other development strategies, for example, coaches, role models, and educational experiences (Cobb & Gibbs, 1990; Morrison & Hock, 1986; Northcraft et al., 1992; Seibert et al., 1995). For example, in a job-swapping program at Greyhound Financial Corporation, managers are coached by the previous job-holder (Northcraft et al., 1992). Motorola uses the classroom environment as a vehicle to prepare for and debrief developmental assignments (Seibert et al., 1995). Furthermore, the development system should be integrated with a reward system that recognizes employees for their learning and development (Cobbs & Gibbs, 1990; Northcraft et al., 1992). Finally, managing a development system requires collaboration and close coordination between line managers and human resources functions (Clark & Lyness, 1991).

We also noted variations across the articles that reflect certain differences in approaches to developmental assignments. First, the time frame in which people stayed in developmental assignments varied in different settings. Some organizations, like Citicorp, take a long-term approach to development (Clark & Lyness, 1991). Within that organization, high-potential managers are appointed to two developmental assignments, each lasting between three and four years. The Greyhound Financial Corporation uses a one-year cycle for assignments (Northcraft et al., 1992). The addition of specific developmental job components, such as writing up a policy statement (Lombardo & Eichinger, 1989), represents the other end of the continuum because of their short-term nature.

One of the most delicate aspects of managing developmental assignments relates to their inherently risky natures. Different "risk taking" philosophies have been used by different organizations. For example, the Oklahoma Department of Corrections uses a relatively safe approach by reducing the accountability of managers placed in developmental assignments (Friedman, 1990). A seemingly riskier approach is taken by Citicorp, which places high-potential managers in developmental assignments for which they are only 60 to 70% qualified (Clark & Lyness, 1991).

The target population of the developmental efforts that use assignments also varies. Some efforts are designed exclusively for high-potential managers (Clark & Lyness, 1991; Northcraft et al., 1992; Seibert et al., 1995), and others are targeted at developing specific skills in a broader cross-section of managers (Cobb & Gibbs, 1990; Friedman, 1990).

The developmental potential of assignments can be enhanced by helping managers learn from experience.

Human resource professionals and management consultants suggest several strategies for improving the job incumbent's ability to learn from his or her job assignment.

1. *Prepare managers for developmental assignments.* A few authors highlight the importance of the planning stage in ensuring the success of developmental assignments. This preparation can take several forms. For one, the learning style of managers can be assessed with instruments such as the *Learning Style Inventory* and the *Learning Styles Questionnaire* (Mumford, 1987). This enables the learning manager to adapt the learning situation to his or her particular style. Dechant (1994) offers a structured exercise to help managers plan and manage a new developmental assignment.

Stewart (1984) suggests that those in charge of implementing developmental assignments be mindful that new job incumbents need to be seen as credible in the eyes of their new co-workers. This can be done by selecting managers with some knowledge of their future co-workers or environment and with experience in at least one key aspect of their new assignment. Furthermore, the management of developmental assignments can include the creation of screening devices for selection and placement of managers to ensure that those given the assignments possess the adequate foundations on which to build the desired skills and abilities (Bonoma & Lawler, 1989; Temporal & Burnett, 1990).

2. *Provide coaching during developmental assignments.* As noted earlier, at Greyhound Financial managers are coached by the previous job-holder (Northcraft et al., 1992). At 3M, high-potential managers in special overseas assignments are supported by a senior, U.S.-based executive. Mumford (1980) and Robinson and Wick (1992) offer numerous strategies for getting advice, feedback, and support from others during a developmental assignment.

3. *Help managers be more reflective and self-aware.* The integration of periodic feedback in the process (Dechant, 1994; Robinson & Wick, 1992), the use of a learning diary (Lombardo & Eichinger, 1989), and the allocation of reflection periods during and after the assignment (Dechant, 1994; Robinson & Wick, 1992) have been used to support learning from developmental assignments. Wick and Léon (1993) and Honey and Mumford (1989) also offer guides for managers interested in taking charge of their development. Their books address the steps that individual managers should take to make the most of their experiences by offering a series of techniques that facilitate learning. They also identify barriers to learning that managers may encounter.

Research Directions

An overview of the articles and books found in this section highlights an obvious dearth of systematic field research on developmental assignments. Although a substantial amount of information has been gathered on individual efforts, most of it is disjointed and lacks a unifying theme. Three basic research questions are suggested by this literature: (1) What factors contribute to the success of developmental assignments? (2) What standards are to be used to assess the outcomes of developmental assignments? (3) What are the indirect effects of implementing developmental assignment systems in organizations? These questions are discussed in the following section.

What factors contribute to the success of developmental assignments?

A variety of efforts using developmental assignments are described in this section. These efforts display a very wide range of characteristics. Organizations, for example, have experimented with varying degree of "stretch" between the employee's skills and abilities and the requirements of the position. In some cases, the stretch is only limited to specific areas (Lombardo & Eichinger, 1989; White, 1992) while others are more involved and cover a broader range of managers' skills and abilities (Seibert et al., 1995). Another difference in approach toward developmental assignments is found in the time frame set for them. In this section, a few authors describe assignments that were framed in very condensed time periods (Friedman, 1990), and others described more lengthy assignments (Clark & Lyness, 1991). There are many other areas in which developmental assignments vary—such as with the use of classroom support and of coaches and mentors—and it is very difficult, at this point, to distinguish which of these factors (or which combination of factors) is important for development. It seems that, for most organizations, using developmental assignments is experimental in nature. A research strategy aimed at optimizing the parameters within which developmental assignments operate would be helpful; this knowledge would assure maximum impact for developmental assignments.

What standards are to be used to assess the outcomes of developmental assignments?

A key aspect of any developmental tool is the evaluation of its impact; this is especially true for a relatively new technique like formal approaches to developmental assignments. Although such assignments are designed for individual development, as described in many annotations, they also involve the accomplishment of a task. The outcomes of developmental assignments can, in other words, be measured at the individual *and* organizational level. Throughout the annotations it was made explicit that for developmental assignments to have an impact at the individual level, they also had to possess organizational significance. These assignments, then, have two purposes: (1) the development of certain skills and abilities for an individual (for example, develop strategic planning abilities), and (2) the accomplishment of certain organizational goals (for example, a start-up assignment in a foreign country). The relationship between these two outcomes is still unclear; can one learn and develop independently from the organizational outcomes of the assignment? In other words, can one learn from an assignment regardless of how well one succeeds in that assignment? Are there specific mechanisms associated with learning from a failed assignment? By the same token, are there mechanisms related with learning from a successful assignment? This knowledge is crucial to optimize the development that can be derived from assignments.

What are the indirect effects of implementing developmental-assignment systems in organizations?

The implementation of developmental assignments is an involved process. Developmental needs have to be identified and matched with appropriate assignments, managers have to be transferred to these new positions, or a new workflow has to be created to supplement existing positions with additional responsibilities. In addition, many organizational initiatives, such as learning-style assessment or the provision of reflection periods, have to be implemented to support the use of developmental assignments. There is a lot of "movement" associated with such an implementation, and the different steps of this process are likely to affect the organization in indirect ways.

For one, the implementation of developmental assignments in organizations may create an artificial distinction between the types of assignments available to the managerial pool. Managers may perceive assignments as either regular or developmental. A potential side effect to this differentiation of assignments is that it assumes that development can only occur in "developmental assignments" and that regular assignments do not offer potential for growth. It would be interesting to investigate how the perceptions of developmental assignments differ from the perceptions of other assignments and what the consequences are of having these two categories of assignments, if any.

Another related issue pertains to the perceptions of nonparticipants. As in any situation in which the number of applicants exceeds the number of positions, some will be left out of the process. Developmental assignments may not be as flexible as traditional training programs when it comes to satisfying the developmental needs of a whole group of managers. It is much easier to schedule another training session than it is to create a new set of assignments or tasks. In most organizations, the number of assignments or tasks to be distributed is limited, and issues of who's in and who's out are likely to surface. These issues are compounded by the fact that those selected will *not*, by definition, be fully qualified for the particular assignment. In this case, the developmental path of one manager may intersect the career path of another, penalizing the latter. Thus, the implementation of developmental assignments needs to be investigated in terms of its impact on all organizational members. Because this developmental system reaches constituencies beyond those whose development is targeted, organization-wide issues are bound to arise and have significant impact on the overall utility of the system.

Annotations

Section 3.1: Systematic and Intentional Uses of Developmental Assignments

Thomas V. Bonoma and Joseph C. Lawler. Chutes and ladders: Growing the general manager. *Sloan Management Review*, 30:3, 1989, pp. 27-37.

The authors outline an organizational framework intended to develop managers through challenging job assignments. This framework involves the implementation of two screening devices, the *up-and-comers screen* and the *general-management screen*, intended to select those managers who might benefit most from developmental job assignments. The purpose of the up-and-comers screen is to identify managers with managerial potential in lower echelons of the organization. Managerial potential, according to the authors, is measured along four dimensions: functional expertise, interest in people, commitment to winning, and creativity. Individuals who possess those characteristics can advance to top levels of the organization and develop another set of abilities, which constitutes the second screening device. These abilities are: sensitivity, perspective, confidence, and good instincts (or "good belly" to use the authors' terminology). It is the organization's responsibility to develop the general-management characteristics in up-and-comers and a list of developmental job assignments is suggested for the development of each. For example, confidence can be built through the expansion of a product in a known market. Other suggestions include the type of supervision desired to build the particular characteristic and the optimal length of the assignment.

Lourine Anderson Clark and Karen S. Lyness. Succession planning as a strategic activity at Citicorp. In L. W. Foster (Ed.), *Advances in applied business strategy* (Vol. 2). Greenwich, CT: JAI Press, 1991, pp. 205-224.

The authors describe how Citicorp attempts to link succession planning and business strategy by involving the same managers in both processes. To do so, the succession planning process is continually reexamined in order to meet changing business needs. Active participation and commitment at all organizational levels is critical: senior management is responsible for words and actions indicating that development is a priority; the human resources function is responsible for creating development plans and ensuring that they are executed; and line management is responsible for identifying talent, executing the plan, and coaching and providing feedback to high-potential managers.

The effort to align succession planning with business strategy was motivated by the tremendous growth, decentralization, and hierarchical flattening that Citicorp experienced in the last few decades. Previous succession planning efforts, in which senior management personally follows the development of their successors, lost most of their effectiveness as Citicorp's workforce surpassed 30,000 employees. At that point, the development of the best and brightest required a more disciplined effort. The dispersion of the organization's strategic centers resulted in separate human resources units, each more concerned with the developmental needs of their own business groups than with global, longer-range issues. This flattening of Citicorp's organizational structure caused a scarcity of general-manager positions at the lower levels of the company. Traditionally, these assignments (for example, start-ups in a foreign country) were perfect developmental opportunities because of the challenge, autonomy, and visibility that they offered. To contend with the emerging organizational structure of Citicorp and the scarcity of "formal" developmental assignments, Citicorp adopted a strategy, relying heavily on developmental assignments, in which succession planning was structured and aligned with the organization's long-term vision.

Citicorp's current plan entails placing high-potentials into jobs for which they are no more than 60 to 70% qualified. The authors caution that, when thinking about stretch assignments, companies need to differentiate "smart" versus "dumb" risks in order to avoid situations in which a person lacks the specific skills that are essential for success in a particular job. Also, Citicorp understands that, although most managers have developmental needs, some skills and abilities are more important than others for the organization; thus, not all needs have to be addressed equally.

A long-term succession planning strategy implemented at Citicorp, called Corporate Property 2000, relies almost entirely on developmental assignments. As stated by the authors, "The purpose of this process is to identify, test, and nurture our best young people to ensure we will have this generation of talent ready for leadership in fifteen to twenty years" (p. 219). After being chosen according to a selective set of criteria, high-potentials are provided with developmental assignments and experiences to help them reach their full potential. During a span of fifteen years, which constitutes the projected length of the developmental plan, participants are assigned to at least two long-term assignments that each last between three and four years. In accordance with Citicorp strategic goals, one of those assignments is designed to develop interpersonal and strategic skills while the other is designed to develop general-management skills. The authors note that the long-term nature of the assignments is deemed very important in order for managers to see the consequences of their decisions and learn from their successes and failures.

Jeremy Cobb and John Gibbs. A new, competency-based, on-the-job programme for developing professional excellence in engineering. *Journal of Management Development*, 9:3, 1990, pp. 60-72.

This article focuses on an on-the-job developmental program undertaken by Mobil Oil Corporation in the early 1980s. As part of their competency-based professional development program for engineers, Mobil initiated a systematic program targeted at fifteen specific engineering competencies. Challenging assignments, role models, and comprehensive coaching were included. In addition, a peripheral structure that allowed for continuous assessment of the competencies, feedback, discussion meetings, developmental plans, and a supplementary resource guide was installed.

The authors offer a series of lessons to be learned from Mobil Oil's success: (1) collaboration between the design and implementation team for the duration of the program; (2) willingness to adapt the program for the target audience; (3) starting the planning of the implementation stage early; (4) implementation of structural support such as forming an implementation committee responsible for monitoring and overseeing the program, holding supervisors accountable for their development efforts, and providing recognition and rewards for development activities; and (5) ensuring the selection of highly-qualified people in the implementation and maintenance role.

Stewart D. Friedman. Succession systems in the public sector: Lessons from the Oklahoma Department of Corrections. *Public Personnel Management*, 19:3, 1990, pp. 291-303.

Friedman describes the succession system in place at the Oklahoma Department of Corrections (DOC). In addition to placing a heavy emphasis on transition training and formal executive training, the DOC uses job placements in combination with job rotations as an integral part of its system. As a rule, the DOC considers job placements as developmental opportunities, which means that there is a certain risk of failure attached to these opportunities. In order to minimize the risk and still reap the benefit of the developmental assignments, people are placed in temporary assignments where accountability and authority are reduced but visibility is still important.

Another important aspect of this program is the structural changes that are made to accommodate the development of decision-making responsibility. The hierarchy of the organization was reorganized in order to provide more authority to a set of lower positions. This change is aimed at creating opportunities for managers to make difficult decisions early in their career, preparing them for senior positions.

Douglas T. Hall. Executive careers and learning: Aligning selection, strategy, and development. *Human Resource Planning*, 18:2, 1995, pp. 14-23.

This paper explains how executive development based on experiential learning can be aligned with the business strategies of organizations. Because most development occurs as a result of on-the-job experiences, the manner by which these experiences is allocated constitutes a very important aspect of the overall development process. The author stresses that the selection for assignments is *a*, if not *the*, critical factor in an individual's development as an executive.

In order to link executive development to business strategy, Hall argues that a clear and well-communicated vision needs to be formulated by top management. From this, specific business needs can be articulated by making assignments that target these needs easier to identify. Although most developmental efforts are strategy-based, this strategy is too often ill defined. By making these implicit strategies explicit, developmental efforts can be oriented more efficiently. Hall offers several ways of linking developmental assignments with business strategy. For instance, "corporate disturbances" can be capitalized on by using real organizational changes as vehicles for learning. Action-learning programs that focus on immediate business issues are another. Also, organizations need to be more efficient at capturing the learning that may have taken place in assignments. For example, the learning from international assignments can be maximized by using back-home mentors to keep tabs on the expatriates.

Hall argues that selection for developmental assignments should be based on strategic needs. This enables top management to devote time and effort to ensure that both the individual and the organization benefit from the assignment. He concludes that the difficulty in "framing" the learning of developmental assignments often results in a disconnect between the goal of these assignments and the overall organizational strategy.

Michael M. Lombardo and Robert W. Eichinger. *Eighty-eight assignments for development in place: Enhancing the developmental challenge of existing jobs.* Greensboro, NC: Center for Creative Leadership, 1989, 29 pages.

The authors state that "challenge and growth can be added to virtually all managerial and physical jobs" (p. 1), and this report provides a tool to facilitate the addition of challenging assignments to existing jobs. Because of the current reality of organizations—the flattening of hierarchy and the increase in downsizing—job changes for developmental purposes are increasingly difficult. On-the-job development, however, can be achieved without complete job changes through the addition of specific challenges.

The authors report the eleven characteristics of challenges most commonly cited by managers: (1) success and failure are both possible and will be obvious to others; (2) requires aggressive individual, "take charge" leadership; (3) involves working with new people; (4) creates additional personal pressure; (5) requires influencing people, activities, and factors over which the manager has no direct authority or control; (6) involves high variety; (7) will be closely watched by people whose opinions count; (8) requires building a team, starting something from scratch, or fixing or turning around a team or an operation or project in trouble; (9) has a major strategic component and is intellectually challenging; (10) involves interacting with an especially good or bad boss; and (11) something important is missing, such as top management support, key skills, credibility, etc.

Some of these challenges occur naturally through a complete job change, however they can also be experienced in existing jobs, through the addition of specific assignments. The authors describe, in a comprehensive table, eighty-eight assignments that contain a different mixture of these eleven challenges. These assignments are classified under five categories: small projects and start-ups, small scope jumps and fix-its, small strategic assignments, coursework/coaching assignments, and off-job activities.

The authors have also organized their findings to enable the reader to target specific developmental needs. For example, the authors recommend that a manager who lacks decisiveness be given an assignment with a deadline (more specific assignments are also suggested). A chart that matches needs with assignments is provided. Finally, the authors present some practical tips to facilitate transitions to new assignments. These suggestions range from pairing up with an experienced other for learning purposes, to keeping a learning diary.

Cynthia D. McCauley, Lorrina J. Eastman, and Patricia J. Ohlott. Linking management selection and development through stretch assignments. *Human Resource Management*, 34:1, 1995, pp. 93-115.

This article provides a framework and suggests strategies for incorporating management development considerations into selection processes. The framework is based on the assumption that on-the-job learning is most likely to occur when managers are faced with challenging situations, and it delineates fifteen developmental components of jobs (features of jobs that represent challenging situations). These components are clustered into five broad categories: transitions, creating change, high level of responsibility, nonauthority relationships, and obstacles.

Data from the *Developmental Challenge Profile (DCP)* are used to illustrate how various types of managerial jobs differ in terms of the fifteen developmental components. Four job situations were examined: moving into a staff position for the first time, moving into a general-management position for the first time, taking over after a job incumbent has been fired, and having an international assignment. Because there were differences in the developmental-component profiles for these four jobs, there were also differences in what managers reported learning. For example, new general managers scored high on components related to creating change and thus reported learning a great deal about recognizing and seizing opportunities.

The authors make several suggestions for including developmental considerations in selection decisions: (1) gather information about the developmental components the incumbent will likely face; (2) consider how the job might offer different types or degrees of stretch for different candidates; (3) find the right balance between matching the manager's talents to the demand of the job and stretching beyond those demands; (4) use ability to learn from experience as a selection criterion; and (5) once a manager has been selected, encourage and support his or her learning from experience. They also argue that a developmentally focused succession-planning system places equal amounts of responsibility for development on the manager and the organization, uses multiple strategies for creating developmental assignments rather than relying primarily on promotions or other major moves, and sees follow-up as an essential part of succession planning. Suggestions and examples for creating this type of focus are presented.

Robert F. Morrison and Roger R. Hock. Career building: Learning from cumulative work experience. In D. T. Hall (Ed.), *Career development in organizations*. San Francisco: Jossey-Bass, 1986, pp. 236-273.

This article outlines the need for organizations to take an active part in career development and provides specific actions by which they can accomplish this. Since on-the-job learning is arguably the main source of development, the authors state that experiences derived from different assignments within an organization need to be systematically assessed and used as part of a long-term plan. They propose an eight-step plan that involves the identification of key organizational positions or families of positions as developmental targets to be used by managers as guides throughout their career progression. (1) Identify key target positions. These positions should be central to the purpose of the organization and also distant enough from entry-level positions to serve as effective goals. (2) Analyze the key target positions to understand the skills, knowledge, and ability that they entail. (3) Identify potential pattern positions. These positions are responsible for channeling managers into the key positions. (4) Establish a hierarchical position or, in other words, order the pattern positions into clusters according to their values to the organization. (5) Analyze the job content and job context of the different clusters. An important dimension is the amount of time required for managers to achieve mastery. (6) Design a developmental career pattern in which job patterns are arranged in growth sequences (namely, particular skills, knowledge, and abilities are hierarchically sequenced according to their complexity). (7) and (8) Assess training requirements and individual potential in order to facilitate and monitor progress.

Gregory B. Northcraft, Terri L. Griffith, and Christina E. Shalley. Building top management muscle in a slow growth environment. *Academy of Management Executive*, 6:1, 1992, pp. 32-40.

The authors outline the implementation of a job rotation program for high-potential executives at Greyhound Financial Corporation. To counteract the lack of upward mobility and the prevalence of career plateauing in the organization, a system of job swapping at high levels was implemented. The program includes a few high-potential executives who change jobs with each other every year. These assignments are characterized by a learning period during which the new managers are coached by previous managers, and a system of compensation in which titles and compensation packages are maintained.

According to the authors, the benefits of this program are numerous. First, it allows for some formal recognition of high-potential managers and prevents stagnation of these individuals. Second, it increases organizational creativity by increasing the base of knowledge that the participants can draw from and by providing the opportunity for participants to try new approaches. Third, the fact that participants become more marketable and might leave the company seemed to be counterbalanced by an increased sense of loyalty toward Greyhound, stemming from participation in the program. Finally, the program strengthened the networks within the company through the coaching between participants and the cooperation between participants and their new subordinates to get the job done.

The authors note the importance of the perceptions of nonparticipants toward the program. A feeling of being passed over might result from having one's supervisor replaced by someone from another department who is less qualified. They suggest implementing this program at multiple levels to circumvent this situation.

Kent W. Seibert, Douglas T. Hall, and Kathy E. Kram. Strengthening the weak link in strategic executive development: Integrating individual development and global business strategy. *Human Resource Management*, 34:4, 1995, pp. 549-567.

The gap between executive development and business strategy that exists in most organizations is examined here. The authors suggest three reasons for the existence of this gap: (1) lack of concern for the customer's needs on the part of the human resources development function, (2) the inability of the human resources function to respond quickly to changing business strategies, and (3) the existence of a false dichotomy between individual development and conducting business.

Nevertheless, the link between development and business strategy is feasible as demonstrated by case studies on 3M Company and Motorola. For 3M, the decision to capture a global market was coupled with an effort to increase their executives' knowledge of global operations (for example, recognizing the importance of understanding overseas markets). The company put in place an overseas assignment, typically running a subsidiary in one country, for high-potential managers who might benefit from the experience. Acceptance of the program was high because managers clearly understood that the assignment was necessary for their career progress and that they would be formally supported in their assignment by a senior U.S.-based executive. The close link between strategy and development is evidenced by the adaptation of the program to the rapidly changing European business environment. In order to develop the ability to manage transitional interdependencies (with the advent of the European Economic Community), 3M swiftly assigned managers to manage a group of products for all Europe.

The Motorola initiative also provides insights on innovative usage of classroom experience to reinforce on-the-job development. The classroom, for Motorola, is seen as a gathering place where managers can prepare for and be debriefed on the developmental experience. During these "classes," managers receive feedback (for developmental purposes only) from other participants; this is seen as an integral part of the overall learning experience.

In sum, this article proposes a new approach for executive development, one whose primary goal is not development but implementation of business strategy through development. The key for this approach is to know enough about the business strategy to be able to find or construct assignments that address key issues. Developmental programs need to be flexible enough to adapt quickly to business changes and also provide for a well-established support structure, such as classroom experience or sponsorship, to foster an environment from which managers can learn from those experiences.

Rosemary Stewart. Developing managers by radical job moves. *Journal of Management Development*, 3:2, 1984, pp. 48-55.

The author reflects on her experience as a consultant with top managers who experienced radical job moves at one point in their careers. First, she contrasts the types of moves that occur in different types of organizations and comments on organizational differences in developmental opportunities. For example, opportunities for developing general managerial skills are more common in decentralized organizations like retail chain stores, because in those types of organizations an individual can easily be moved to manage a discrete unit. More integrated organizations tend to offer fewer opportunities for a gradual development of general managerial skills; the move there is often a drastic one, from a technical assignment to a major managerial assignment.

Second, Stewart contrasts the competencies developed in three common job moves: (1) direct promotions constitute increases in responsibility and ambiguity; (2) line-to-staff moves expose managers to different types of relationships, different patterns of work, and also constitutes an increase in responsibility; and (3) cross-functional moves present a change in job content and knowledge.

Stewart recommends a set of organizational policies for using job experience as part of the managerial development effort. For one, organizations need to understand which jobs possess developmental potential and how movement from one job to another contributes to managers' development. Second, steps need to be taken in order for "job movers" to be seen as credible in the eyes of their future co-workers; support from all organizational members is very important given the risky nature of these assignments. The credibility is more likely to be present, the author recommends, if one of the following attributes is present in "job movers": experience with the business-related tasks required for the position, knowledge of future co-workers, or experience in one of the key disciplines for that position.

Randall P. White. Job as classroom: Using assignments to leverage development. In D. H. Montross & C. J. Shinkman (Eds.), *Career development: Theory and practice.* Springfield, IL: Charles C. Thomas, 1992, pp. 190-206.

On-the-job development is offered here as an effective tool to move promising managers into the executive suite and as a remedy to the flattening of organizations and the need to develop managerial skills earlier in one's career. This chapter builds on the research conducted at the Center for Creative Leadership focusing on experiential learning and identifies five broad categories of assignments that were considered developmental by managers. The assignment categories are fix-it/turnaround, starting from scratch, scope changes, line-to-staff, and special projects/task forces.

The author proposes different mechanisms by which human resources professionals can use the implications of these findings. The first is to conduct a multilevel survey to identify the developmental characteristics of each job, the characteristics of the job holders in terms of track record and background, and the learning that takes place in those jobs, if any. An alternative is to interview senior management in order to determine which assignment(s) contributed to their development.

An illustration of how this process was implemented in a large organization is provided. The creation of an *experience-by-learning* matrix, using a survey methodology, allows organizational members to clearly see what knowledge, skills, and abilities will result from specific assignments.

A few caveats are offered to help maximize learning through developmental assignments. First, organizations have to find ways to provide support for individuals who are doing developmental assignments. Second, the success of developmental assignments is contingent upon the individual's desire to learn. Finally, the author notes that developmental assignments need not necessarily involve complete reassignments but can be implemented through the addition of specific developmental responsibilities to an existing position.

Section 3.2: Helping Managers Learn from Experience

Kathleen Dechant. Making the most of job assignments: An exercise in planning for learning. *Journal of Management Education*, 18:2, 1994, pp. 198-211.

This paper offers a practical exercise, based on the author's model of learning, by which managers (in this case executive MBA students) can anticipate and monitor the learning process that takes place in a developmental job assignment. The proposed model is composed of four components: learning inputs, learning strategies, feedback, and learning outcomes. Individuals who foresee a developmental assignment are asked to lay out, according to four established dimensions, what they know about the new assignment (learning inputs). Following this, a list of learning needs is created. This stage is the most important since the strategy needs to address the learning needs of everybody involved with that new assignment. A strategy to gather feedback relating to the effectiveness of the learning strategy is then drafted, usually involving the participant's immediate network (peers and supervisor). The last component requires the participant to reflect on the individual and organizational outcomes of the learning strategy.

A worksheet designed to guide participants through the four stages is provided.

Peter Honey and Alan Mumford. *The manual of learning opportunities*. Peter Honey, Publisher, Ardingly House, 10 Linden Avenue, Maidenhead, Berkshire, England, SL6 6HB, 1989.

This manual offers a practical guide to learning from experience. The basic argument presented here is that everything that happens is a learning opportunity. However, to ensure learning, individuals have to recognize these opportunities *and* make use of them; those who succeed in doing both are "learning opportunists." Using an extensive theoretical foundation, the authors provide specific exercises, questionnaires, and checklists to support one's development into a learning opportunist. This hands-on material can be used to help with individual development efforts, as part of developmental workshops or as diagnosis tools for the learning organization.

Most of this manual revolves around the *Learning Diagnostic Questionnaire (LDQ)*, presented in Section 2; it is an instrument designed to complement the author's previous instrument, the *Learning Styles Questionnaire (LSQ)*. As with the *LSQ*, the *LDQ* measures learning preferences or learning style. However, the authors recognize that learning preference is only part of the story. With the *LDQ*, situational and motivational components of learning are also addressed; these components are labeled *Working Situation* and *Attitudes and Emotions*. Based on this instrument, an individual's effectiveness in recognizing and acting on learning opportunities is assessed.

Section 3 presents the Learning Cycle (see Mumford, 1995) and the different approaches to learning. Section 4 offers a series of developmental opportunities that can be added to existing jobs. For example, the assignment to projects with clear developmental objectives represents an excellent learning stimulus. An exercise designed to reflect on past opportunities that may or may not have been useful is provided at the end of the section.

Section 5, called Transformational Learning Opportunities, deals with the opportunities offered by a new position. This section also includes two exercises designed to facilitate learning from a new position. Section 6 focuses on the factors influencing learning. Four factors are identified: job content, organizational environment, personal factors, and the learning process. Three exercises designed to identify and improve these four factors are described.

Section 7 presents the attitudinal and emotional influences of learning, both of which play a major part in learning from experience. For example, the authors outline how different emotions can interfere with each of the four stages of the learning cycle. Feelings of fear, failure, and anxiety can often prevent one to engage in stage 1, which represents having a developmental experience. One can overcome these influences by consciously going against them and creating an environment that reinforces and encourages taking advantage of learning opportunities.

In Section 8 the authors provide material that helps people identify the skills of learning and develop them. Strategies associated with learning logs, learning within groups, and learning reviews are described. Three exercises (each with multiple variations) designed to help with the identification and development of learning skills are offered. Section 9 describes how to identify and use various people as helpers in one's learning process. At the end of the section, six exercises are proposed to facilitate the identification of helpers and to make use of them.

Alan Mumford. *Making experience pay*. Berkshire, England: McGraw-Hill, 1980, 184 pages.

This book is designed to help managers direct their own learning by making the most of opportunities in their environments. In the first chapter, in which he outlines the range of influences on managers' opportunities to learn on the job, Mumford argues that most learning opportunities occur in managers' natural environment. Most occur as a combination of factors such as bosses, colleagues, organizational structure, and organizational climate converge to create learning environments. Mumford also acknowledges the home environment as a powerful learning context.

In chapter two, the author emphasizes the need for managers to recognize and use learning opportunities present in their existing jobs. This process involves defining their jobs objectively (time spent on different tasks) and subjectively (through the eyes of others) and identifying areas in need of development. Although many factors are known to influence the learning process, Mumford points out that the responsibility for learning ultimately falls to the manager. An important step in learning from experience, described in chapter three, is the assessment of one's personal effectiveness and the identification of learning needs through appraisal discussions with peers or supervisors or self-appraisals.

In chapter four, Mumford acknowledges the abundance of learning theories. He chooses to concentrate on three theories that are most relevant to experiential learning: *behavioral learning theory*, which emphasizes the role of the environment on learning; *experiential learning theory*, which focuses on the involvement of the whole person (this chapter includes a description of David Kolb's learning styles); and *cognitive learning theory*, which concentrates on learning through reflection and careful analysis of experience. This chapter also outlines the motivational aspect of learning on the job.

Chapter five focuses on the uniqueness of the learning manager and the need for directing his or her own learning instead of it being influenced by external factors. Mumford describes the skills involved in effective learning behavior, such as the ability to identify learning needs, the ability to measure effectiveness, and the ability to accept help and share information with others.

In chapter six, differences among the different learning opportunities available to managers are distinguished. Unplanned learning through a current job involves the kind of experiences that are recognized as being developmental only after the fact. In contrast, planned learning can be experienced through the addition of developmental components, special assignments, or experience outside of work. The author stresses how difficult it is for managers to recognize opportunities in their world. For example, overreliance on formal training and increased activity may result in failure to recognize learning opportunities on the job.

Chapter seven provides examples of learning through job experiences, both planned and unplanned. In chapter eight, Mumford describes how opportunities can most effectively be turned into learning results. For this transfer to occur, the manager must first recognize that an opportunity exists; must have the capacity to recognize that learning is not a discrete activity, separate from normal tasks; must review the resources and support available; and should understand the benefit of specifying learning objectives and measuring success in achieving them. The author offers a rational approach to this process that consists of collecting data on one's learning needs, planning, evaluating, and so forth. Another approach focuses on sharing the learning process with others (for instance, boss and peers) to obtain feedback and support. Chapter nine focuses on the usage of formal courses and how managers can make the most of these learning experiences. The final chapter shows how managers may be helped by people other than bosses and colleagues.

Alan Mumford. Helping managers learn to learn: Using learning styles and learning biography. *Journal of Management Development*, 6:5, 1987, pp. 49-60.

In this article, the author describes some of the techniques and processes available to facilitate the implementation of developmental programs based on experiential learning. First and most important, the author argues that participants need to be fully aware of the purpose of the development initiative. They are to play an active part in their own development. While Mumford offers a critique of the *Learning Style Indicator (LSI)* and the *Learning Styles Questionnaire (LSQ)* as instruments to be used in development programs, the crux of this article lies in the description of two training approaches aimed at learning to learn from experience. The first approach is centered around the assessment of one's learning style (with the *LSI* or the *LSQ*). The basic process involves the administration of the instrument by a trainer followed by a series of group discussions and development planning. The second approach does not rely on learning-styles instruments but involves discussions that focus on the identification of successful and unsuccessful past experience, the identification of barriers to personal learning, and the development of a personal learning plan. The author provides a series of four case studies of learning-to-learn programs.

Gail S. Robinson and Calhoun W. Wick. Executive development that makes a business difference. *Human Resource Planning*, 15:1, 1992, pp. 63-76.

This article offers a framework, based on the authors' research and consulting experience, for executive development through experience. According to this framework, a developmental experience is one that is characterized by challenge, novelty, responsibility, and choice. In order to derive positive outcomes from those experiences they have to be handled with certain learning strategies, mainly critical thinking, hypothesis testing, and critical reflection. Personal characteristics associated with these strategies are cognitive complexity, tolerance for ambiguity, and flexibility.

The authors propose three basic elements of a successful developmental experience. First, a planning period is helpful to prepare individuals for the experience, especially for those areas where stretch and growth is expected. Second, a repetitive cycle of action and reflection should be in place for individual learners. Peer groups, reflection periods, coaching, and just-in-time training provide feedback and emotional support *during* the developmental experience. Finally, a reflection period after the experience allows for a more objective and global view of the experience.

A description of a practice-based program is provided. In addition, two case studies are offered to demonstrate the significant impact that learning from experience can have when aligned with business goals.

Paul Temporal and Ken Burnett. Strategic corporate assignments and international management development. *Journal of Management Development*, 9:5, 1990, pp. 58-64.

This article focuses on a specific effort, undertaken by an international company to develop an international manager. The authors state that the advent of mergers, acquisitions, and the overall globalization process has led to a growing emphasis on international management abilities. They claim that the field of management development is lagging behind this trend and is currently ill equipped to supply these skills. A popular development strategy involves assigning managers to a new market entry in a foreign country. Such assignments are believed to provide managers with exposure to the technical and cultural complexity of international management. However, when these assignments result in financial losses, it can be very costly. A case study of a start-up assignment in an Asian country that resulted in financial losses and the reassignment of the manager illustrates some of the pitfalls involved in such a developmental strategy.

The authors provide a list of actions taken by the manager in the case study and reasons for his failure. A "learning review" was conducted by the company to understand the experience. This review yielded several organizational learnings. (1) International assignments provide a rich developmental experience. (2) They can be extremely costly if conducted without adequate training and developmental assistance. (3) Preparation for those assignments is needed on two fronts: technical competencies and cultural competencies. Several microstrategies are proposed to bring managers up to speed before they start their assignments. (4) Developmental efforts should be structured to track the learning progress of managers. These monitoring structures, however, should not discourage the experiential nature of the assignment. (5) Developmental efforts that rely on country-specific experiences need to also incorporate global organizational issues as part of the assignment. (6) Managers selected for such assignments need to be well versed in the corporate culture and be mindful that this culture may need adjustments for it to fit the culture of the host country.

The authors provide an extensive checklist of questions to guide the use of international assignments for development purposes.

Calhoun W. Wick and Lu Stanton León. *The learning edge: How smart managers and smart companies stay ahead.* New York: McGraw-Hill, 1993, 232 pages.

This book is designed to facilitate the application of on-the-job learning concepts for individuals and organizations. The first part of the book emphasizes the importance of learning on the job. The authors offer the results of their research efforts, based on over 900 managers from Fortune 500 companies, to support their statement. Their research yielded seven "discoveries" about on-the-job learning and development: (1) development occurs on the job; (2) bad bosses can be beneficial; (3) individual initiative and choice are critical to development; (4) there is no mandatory age for learning; (5) development does not always feel good; (6) development does not occur overnight; and (7) key elements for growth are challenge, novelty, relationships, and responsibility.

The second part of the book focuses on taking charge of one's development. They propose a sequential model of five steps, labeled S.M.A.R.T. (Select, Map, Act, Review, Target), that are designed to facilitate the learning process for individual managers. As an example, step 1 consists of selecting a learning goal that is vital to the manager and his or her company. To supplement this model, a series of five techniques or "power tools" for learning are also offered. A whole chapter is used to cover such techniques as visualization to promote learning, and the "learning star," a diagnostic tool for learning patterns. In addition, the authors identify a series of ten barriers to learning on-the-job followed by practical steps to circumvent them. For example, managers often mention that the time required to commit fully to one's development is simply not available to them. To counter this adverse situation, managers can delegate some of their work or block off some time for learning.

The last section of the book expands the concept of learning and development to the organization as a whole. The authors propose a formula for the learning organization, which includes having the following: a leader with a clear vision, a detailed action plan, rapid sharing of information, inventiveness, and the ability to implement the plan. A whole chapter is devoted to the role of the leader in those organizations. The authors also provide detailed descriptions of five organizations in which "learning is in high gear," such as Corning, Eastman Kodak Company, and Motorola.

Connections

Action Learning

Action-learning programs are typically characterized by individual managers working together in small groups to solve real problems. These programs are based on Revans' (1980) original ideas regarding management education. The original design for action-learning programs revolved around the premise that managers learn better from practical experiences and each other than from formal training. Such programs are fairly structured in terms of process, have a set duration, and are frequently part of a larger organizational development effort. Many published articles have focused on action-learning techniques and programs. Most of this literature is found in the popular press, and the majority of articles are descriptive or instructional in nature. Specifically, most of these articles describe case studies of action-learning programs developed within organizations, universities, or consulting groups (Braddick, 1988; Clover, 1991; Froiland, 1994; Hurley & Cunningham, 1993; Kable, 1989; Larson, 1986; Lewis & Marsh, 1987; MacNamara, 1985; Marsick, 1990; Mumford, 1991; Newell, Wolf, & Drexler, 1988; Noel & Charan, 1988; Prideaux & Ford, 1988; Robinson & Wick, 1992; Seekings, 1987; Taylor, 1992; Watkins & Marsick, 1993; Wills, 1986).

W. A. G. Braddick. How top managers really learn. *Journal of Management Development*, 7:4, 1988, pp. 55-62.

David Casey. Breaking the shell that encloses your understanding. *Journal of Management Development*, 6:2, 1987, pp. 30-37.

William H. Clover. At TRW, executive training contributes to quality. *Human Resources Professional*, 3:2, 1991, pp. 16-20.

Paul Froiland. Action learning: Taming real problems in real time. *Training*, 31:1, 1994, pp. 27-34.

Bob Garratt. Learning is the core of organizational survival: Action learning is the key integrating process. *Journal of Management Development*, 6:2, 1987, pp. 38-44.

Iain Henderson. Action learning: A missing link in management development? *Personnel Review*, 22:6, 1993, pp. 14-24.

Brian Hurley and Ian Cunningham. Imbibing a new way of learning. *Personnel Management*, 25:3, 1993, pp. 42-45.

James Kable. Management development through action learning. *Journal of Management Development*, 8:2, 1989, pp. 77-80.

Dennis C. Kinlaw. Teaming up for management training. *Training & Development Journal*, 41:11, 1987, pp. 44-46.

Lars Larson. Improving management development through small problem-solving groups. *Journal of Management Development*, 5:2, 1986, pp. 15-26.

John Lawrie. Take action to change performance. *Personnel Journal*, 68:1, 1989, pp. 58-69.

Alec Lewis and Wyndham Marsh. Action learning: The development of field managers in the Prudential Assurance Company. *Journal of Management Development*, 6:2, 1987, pp. 45-56.

Margaret MacNamara. Action learning and organizational development. *Organization Development Journal*, 3:2, 1985, pp. 10-15.

Margaret MacNamara and William H. Weekes. The action learning model of experiential learning for developing managers. *Human Relations*, 35:10, 1982, pp. 879-902.

Charles J. Margerison. Action learning and excellence in management development. *Journal of Management Development*, 7:5, 1988, pp. 43-53.

Victoria Marsick. Experience-based learning: Executive learning outside the classroom. *Journal of Management Development*, 9:4, 1990, pp. 50-60.

John Morris. Action learning: Reflections on a process. *Journal of Management Development*, 6:2, 1987, pp. 57-70.

Alan Mumford. Learning in action. *Personnel Management*, 23:7, 1991, pp. 34-37.

Terry Newell, James Wolf, and Allan Drexler. Rescuing training: Joining learning and application in a federal agency training program. *Public Personnel Management*, 17:3, 1988, pp. 303- 313.

James L. Noel and Ram Charan. Leadership development at GE's Crotonville. *Human Resource Management*, 27:4, 1988, pp. 433-447.

S. Prideaux and James E. Ford. Management development: Competencies, teams, learning contracts and work experience based learning. *Journal of Management Development*, 7:3, 1988, pp. 13-21.

Joseph A. Raelin and Michele LeBien. Learn by doing. *HR Magazine*, 38:2, 1993, pp. 61-70.

Rafael Ramirez. Action learning: A strategic approach for organizations facing turbulent conditions. *Human Relations*, 36:8, 1983, pp. 725-742.

Reginald W. Revans. *Action learning: New techniques for management.* London: Blond & Briggs, 1980, 320 pages.

Reginald W. Revans. Action learning and the cowboys. *Organization Development Journal*, 4:3, 1986, pp. 71-80.

Marshall Sashkin and Steve Franklin. Anticipatory team learning: What is it and how does it happen? *Journal of Management Development*, 12:6, 1993, pp. 34-43.

David Seekings. Allied Irish Bank in Britain: Organizational and business development through action learning. *Leadership & Organization Development Journal*, 8:5, 1987, pp. 26-31.

Stephen Skomp. An introduction to the elements and process of action learning. *Organization Development Journal*, 3:2, 1985, pp. 6-9.

Barry Smith. Mutual mentoring on projects—a proposal to combine the advantages of several established management development methods. *Journal of Management Development*, 9:1, 1990, pp. 51- 57.

Barry Smith. 'Building managers from the inside out': Developing managers through competency-based action learning. *Journal of Management Development*, 12:1, 1993, pp. 43-48.

Sally Taylor. Managing a learning environment. *Personnel Management*, 24:10, 1992, pp. 54-57.

Albert A. Vicere. The changing paradigm for executive development. *Journal of Management Development*, 10:3, 1991, pp. 44-47.

Gordon Wills. The customer first/faculty last approach to excellence. *Journal of Management Development*, 5:4, 1986, pp. 61-68.

Author Index

Title Index

CENTER FOR CREATIVE LEADERSHIP PUBLICATIONS

SELECTED REPORTS:

The Adventures of Team Fantastic: A Practical Guide for Team Leaders and Members
G.L. Hallam (1996, Stock #172) $20.00
CEO Selection: A Street-smart Review G.P. Hollenbeck (1994, Stock #164) $25.00
Choosing 360: A Guide to Evaluating Multi-rater Feedback Instruments for Management
Development E. Van Velsor, J. Brittain Leslie, & J.W. Fleenor (1997, Stock #334) $15.00
Creativity in the R&D Laboratory T.M. Amabile & S.S. Gryskiewicz (1987, Stock #130) $12.00
A Cross-National Comparison of Effective Leadership and Teamwork: Toward a Global
Workforce J.B. Leslie & E. Van Velsor (1998, Stock #177) $15.00
Eighty-eight Assignments for Development in Place: Enhancing the Developmental Challenge
of Existing Jobs M.M. Lombardo & R.W. Eichinger (1989, Stock #136) $15.00
Enhancing 360-degree Feedback for Senior Executives: How to Maximize the Benefits and
Minimize the Risks R.E. Kaplan & C.J. Palus (1994, Stock #160) $15.00
Evolving Leaders: A Model for Promoting Leadership Development in Programs C.J. Palus &
W.H. Drath (1995, Stock #165) $15.00
Forceful Leadership and Enabling Leadership: You Can Do Both R.E. Kaplan (1996, Stock #171) $15.00
Formal Mentoring Programs in Organizations: An Annotated Bibliography C.A. Douglas
(1997, Stock #332) $20.00
Four Essential Ways that Coaching Can Help Executives R. Witherspoon & R.P. White (1997,
Stock #175) $10.00
Gender Differences in the Development of Managers: How Women Managers Learn From
Experience E. Van Velsor & M. W. Hughes (1990, Stock #145) $35.00
A Glass Ceiling Survey: Benchmarking Barriers and Practices A.M. Morrison, C.T. Schreiber,
& K.F. Price (1995, Stock #161) $15.00
Helping Leaders Take Effective Action: A Program Evaluation D.P. Young & N.M. Dixon
(1996, Stock #174) $18.00
How to Design an Effective System for Developing Managers and Executives M.A. Dalton &
G.P. Hollenbeck (1996, Stock #158) $15.00
Inside View: A Leader's Observations on Leadership W.F. Ulmer, Jr. (1997, Stock #176) $12.00
The Intuitive Pragmatists: Conversations with Chief Executive Officers J.S. Bruce (1986,
Stock #310) $12.00
Leadership for Turbulent Times L.R. Sayles (1995, Stock #325) $15.00
A Look at Derailment Today: North America and Europe J. Brittain Leslie & E. Van Velsor
(1996, Stock #169) $20.00
Making Common Sense: Leadership as Meaning-making in a Community of Practice
W.H. Drath & C.J. Palus (1994, Stock #156) $15.00
Management Development through Job Experiences: An Annotated Bibliography
C.D. McCauley & S. Brutus (1998, Stock #337) $20.00
Managerial Promotion: The Dynamics for Men and Women M.N. Ruderman, P.J. Ohlott, &
K.E. Kram (1996, Stock #170) $15.00
Managing Across Cultures: A Learning Framework M.S. Wilson, M.H. Hoppe, & L.R. Sayles
(1996, Stock #173) $15.00
Perspectives on Dialogue: Making Talk Developmental for Individuals and Organizations
N.M. Dixon (1996, Stock #168) $20.00
Preventing Derailment: What To Do Before It's Too Late M.M. Lombardo & R.W. Eichinger
(1989, Stock #138) $25.00
The Realities of Management Promotion M.N. Ruderman & P.J. Ohlott (1994, Stock #157) $15.00
Selection at the Top: An Annotated Bibliography V.I. Sessa & R.J. Campbell (1997, Stock #333) ... $20.00
Should 360-degree Feedback Be Used Only for Developmental Purposes? D.W. Bracken,
M.A. Dalton, R.A. Jako, C.D. McCauley, V.A. Pollman, with Preface by G.P. Hollenbeck (1997,
Stock #335) $15.00
Succession Planning: An Annotated Bibliography L.J. Eastman (1995, Stock #324) $20.00
Training for Action: A New Approach to Executive Development R.M. Burnside &
V.A. Guthrie (1992, Stock #153) $15.00
Twenty-two Ways to Develop Leadership in Staff Managers R.W. Eichinger & M.M. Lombardo
(1990, Stock #144) $15.00

Using 360-degree Feedback in Organizations: An Annotated Bibliography J.W. Fleenor & J.M. Prince (1997, Stock #338) $15.00
Using an Art Technique to Facilitate Leadership Development C. De Ciantis (1995, Stock #166) ... $15.00
Why Managers Have Trouble Empowering: A Theoretical Perspective Based on Concepts of Adult Development W.H. Drath (1993, Stock #155) $15.00

SELECTED BOOKS:

Balancing Act: How Managers Can Integrate Successful Careers and Fulfilling Personal Lives J.R. Kofodimos (1993, Stock #247) $28.00
Beyond Ambition: How Driven Managers Can Lead Better and Live Better R.E. Kaplan, W.H. Drath, & J.R. Kofodimos (1991, Stock #227) $32.95
Breaking Free: A Prescription for Personal and Organizational Change D.M. Noer (1997, Stock #271) $25.00
Breaking the Glass Ceiling: Can Women Reach the Top of America's Largest Corporations? (Updated Edition) A.M. Morrison, R.P. White, & E. Van Velsor (1992, Stock #236A) $13.00
Choosing to Lead (Second Edition) K.E. Clark & M.B. Clark (1996, Stock #327) $25.00
Discovering Creativity: Proceedings of the 1992 International Creativity and Innovation Networking Conference S.S. Gryskiewicz (Ed.) (1993, Stock #319) $30.00
Executive Selection: A Look at What We Know and What We Need to Know D.L. DeVries (1993, Stock #321) $20.00
Healing the Wounds: Overcoming the Trauma of Layoffs and Revitalizing Downsized Organizations D.M. Noer (1993, Stock #245) $29.50
High Flyers: Developing the Next Generation of Leaders M.W. McCall, Jr. (1997, Stock #293) $27.95
If I'm In Charge Here, Why Is Everybody Laughing? D.P. Campbell (1984, Stock #205) $9.95
If You Don't Know Where You're Going You'll Probably End Up Somewhere Else D.P. Campbell (1974, Stock #203) $9.95
Inklings: Collected Columns on Leadership and Creativity D.P. Campbell (1992, Stock #233) $15.00
Leadership: Enhancing the Lessons of Experience (Second Edition) R.L. Hughes, R.C. Ginnett, & G.J. Curphy (1996, Stock #266) $55.00
The Lessons of Experience: How Successful Executives Develop on the Job M.W. McCall, Jr., M.M. Lombardo, & A.M. Morrison (1988, Stock #211) $27.50
Making Diversity Happen: Controversies and Solutions A.M. Morrison, M.N. Ruderman, & M. Hughes-James (1993, Stock #320) $20.00
Maximizing the Value of 360-degree Feedback W.W. Tornow, M. London, & CCL Associates (1998, Stock #295) $42.95
The New Leaders: Guidelines on Leadership Diversity in America A.M. Morrison (1992, Stock #238) $32.00
Readings in Innovation S.S. Gryskiewicz & D.A. Hills (Eds.) (1992, Stock #240) $25.00
Selected Research on Work Team Diversity M.N. Ruderman, M.W. Hughes-James, & S.E. Jackson (Eds.) (1996, Stock #326) $24.95
Staying on Track L.D. Coble & D.L. Brubaker (1997, Stock #280) $18.95
Take the Road to Creativity and Get Off Your Dead End D.P. Campbell (1977, Stock #204) $9.95
The Working Leader: The Triumph of High Performance Over Conventional Management Principles L.R. Sayles (1993, Stock #243) $27.95

SPECIAL PACKAGES:

Development and Derailment (Stock #702; includes 136, 138, & 144) $35.00
The Diversity Collection (Stock #708; includes 145, 177, 236A, 238, 317, & 320) $85.00
Executive Selection (Stock #710; includes 141, 321, 333, & 157) $50.00
Gender Research (Stock #716; includes 145, 161, 170, 236A, & 238) $90.00
HR Professional's Info Pack (Stock #717; includes 136, 158, 165, 169, 324, & 334) $75.00
New Understanding of Leadership (Stock #718; includes 156, 165, & 168) $40.00
Personal Growth, Taking Charge, and Enhancing Creativity (Stock #231; includes 203, 204, & 205) $20.00

Discounts are available. Please write for a comprehensive Publications catalog. Address your request to: Publication, Center for Creative Leadership, P.O. Box 26300, Greensboro, NC 27438-6300, 336-545-2805, or fax to 336-545-3221. All prices subject to change.

ORDER FORM

Or E-mail your order via the Center's online bookstore at www.ccl.org

Name _____ Title _____

Organization _____

Mailing Address _____
(street address required for mailing)

City/State/Zip _____

Telephone _____ FAX _____
(telephone number required for UPS mailing)

Quantity	Stock No.	Title	Unit Cost	Amount

CCL's Federal ID Number
is 237-07-9591.

Subtotal	
Shipping and Handling (add 6% of subtotal with a $4.00 minimum; add 40% on all international shipping)	
NC residents add 6% sales tax; CA residents add 7.75% sales tax; CO residents add 6.2% sales tax	
TOTAL	

METHOD OF PAYMENT
(ALL orders for less than $100 must be PREPAID.)

❏ Check or money order enclosed (payable to Center for Creative Leadership).

❏ Purchase Order No. _____ (Must be accompanied by this form.)

❏ Charge my order, plus shipping, to my credit card:
        ❏ American Express ❏ Discover ❏ MasterCard ❏ VISA

ACCOUNT NUMBER:_____ EXPIRATION DATE: MO.____ YR.____

NAME OF ISSUING BANK: _____

SIGNATURE _____

❏ Please put me on your mailing list.

Publication • Center for Creative Leadership • P.O. Box 26300
Greensboro, NC 27438-6300
336-545-2805 • FAX 336-545-3221

fold here

PLACE
STAMP
HERE

CENTER FOR CREATIVE LEADERSHIP
PUBLICATION
P.O. Box 26300
Greensboro, NC 27438-6300